Divine

HEAVENLY CHOCOLATE RECIPES
WITH A HEART

First published in Great Britain
in 2007 by

Absolute Press
Scarborough House
29 James Street West
Bath BA1 2BT
Phone 44 (0) 1225 316013
Fax 44 (0) 1225 445836
E-mail info@absolutepress.co.uk
Website www.absolutepress.co.uk

Publisher Jon Croft
Editor Meg Avent
Designer Matt Inwood
Publishing Assistant Meg Devenish
Photographer Lisa Barber
Props Stylist Sue Rowlands
Food Stylist Linda Tubby

ISBN 13: 9781904573739

Printed and bound by
1010 Printing International

**TO FIND OUT ALL ABOUT DIVINE
AND WHERE YOU CAN BUY IT VISIT
WWW.DIVINECHOCOLATE.COM**

Every Divine product carries the Fairtrade Mark. This is an independent
guarantee from the Fairtrade Foundation that the chocolate is made with cocoa
beans bought under internationally agreed Fairtrade terms and conditions.
For more information about Fairtrade visit www.fairtrade.org.uk.

Divine Chocolate and its partners
www.divinechocolate.com
www.dubble.co.uk
www.twin.org.uk
www.christian-aid.org.uk
www.comicrelief.com
www.oikocredit.org

Linda Collister's acknowledgements
I would like to thank the many people who helped with this book:
Charlotte Borger and Sophi Tranchell at Divine Chocolate;
Jon Croft, Meg Avent, Matt Inwood and Meg Devenish at Absolute Press;
Lisa Barber, Linda Tubby, Sue Rowlands for photography and styling;
my agent, Barbara Levy; Simon Silverwood; and Dan, Stevie and Alan Hertz.

Photo credits
All images Lisa Barber except pages 8–9 (all © Brian Moody) and pages
12–14 (© Pete Pattison, Brian Moody, Jacqui Macdonald, Louise Taplin
and Karen Robinson)

A note about the text
This book was set using Helvetica Neue and Copperplate Gothic.
Helvetica was designed in 1957 by Max Miedinger of the Swiss-based Haas
foundry. In the early 1980s, Linotype redrew the entire Helvetica family.
The result was Helvetica Neue. Copperplate Gothic was designed in 1901
by Frederic W. Goudy. At first glance it looks like a sans serif font, but small,
pointed serifs lend a discreet and elegant finishing touch.

HEAVENLY CHOCOLATE RECIPES
WITH A HEART

RECIPES BY
LINDA COLLISTER

ABSOLUTE PRESS

THIS BOOK IS DEDICATED TO
THE FARMERS OF KUAPA KOKOO
IN GHANA, WHOSE HARD WORK,
AND AMAZING CO-OPERATIVE SPIRIT
ENSURES THEIR COCOA IS THE
'BEST OF THE BEST' AND PUTS
THE HEAVENLY HEART IN DIVINE.

CONTENTS

FOREWORD

AN IRRESISTIBLE INDULGENCE

Chocolate has an irresistible allure. Those smooth brown slabs of sweetness hold millions in their thrall; the dark velvety sheen of chocolate ganache icing poured over rich chocolate cake draws eyes to patisserie windows, and fingers into mixing bowls all over the developed world. Even the word chocolate – evolved from the Aztec 'xocolatl' cocoa drink – has us transfixed, conjuring the prospect of indulgence as we roll each well-loved syllable on our tongues.

From the first chocolate button to the finest hand-made selection, chocolate has us deliciously hooked – it's a life-long love affair.

The history of how we came to love chocolate is well told elsewhere, and not what makes this book special. This Divine chocolate recipe book is not only a glorious celebration of cooking with chocolate, but also a tribute to the people behind its essential exotic ingredient – cocoa. At the heart of Divine is the pleasure of sharing good chocolate, while guaranteeing cocoa farmers a fair share in it too.

THE DIVINE STORY

Divine's story is the inspiring account of how cocoa farmers came to own a chocolate company, which secured them a fairer deal for their cocoa, and a slice of the much more lucrative chocolate market.

The story starts in Ghana in 1879, when Tetteh Quarshie first brought cocoa there from Equatorial Guinea. Since then, Ghanaian cocoa has developed a global reputation for its quality and taste. Today it is one of the country's main exports. In Ghana, cocoa is mostly grown on small family-owned farms, rather than on large plantations, as cocoa grows best in the humid, shady conditions provided by the rainforest canopy.

Cocoa farming is a precarious business. The trees are vulnerable to various diseases and, although chocolate is one of the world's favourite treats, the world price for cocoa often dips below the level at which it pays enough for small scale farmers to survive.

In 1993, in order to gain more power in an industry where their voice was not being heard, a group of Ghanaian cocoa farmers got together and set up their own cooperative, Kuapa Kokoo. Kuapa aimed to produce the 'best of the best' cocoa, and to work for a better future for its members. At their AGM in 1997 the farmers voted to set up their own Fairtrade chocolate company in the UK – and with investment from The Body Shop and Twin Trading, and the support of Christian Aid and Comic Relief, Divine Chocolate was born.

The recipe for Divine was carefully crafted from the best totally natural ingredients to create a chocolate everybody could love – and the aim of the brand from the very start has been to be pioneering, popular, and absolutely delicious. It is a brand that has won the hearts and minds of chocolate lovers who want to indulge their passion, and support a fairer way of trading.

Images overleaf (the story of the Kuapa Kokoo bean):

Left, top: *Cutting down the ripened cocoa pods*
Left, middle: *Splitting the pods open with a cutlass*
Left, bottom: *Extracting all the beans*
Centre, top: *Wrapping the beans in banana leaves to ferment*
Centre, middle: *Drying and turning the beans in the sun*
Centre, bottom: *Taking the beans to be weighed by the Recorder*
Right, top: *Piling the sacks up at the depot*
Right, middle: *Checking the quality of the beans*
Right, bottom: *A regional Kuapa Kokoo office*

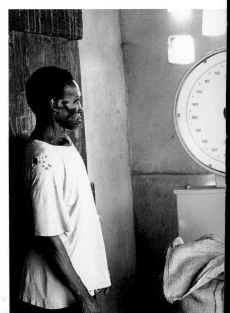

KUAPA KOKOO LTD
NEW-KOFORIDUA

KUAPA KOKOO
SOCIETY
P. O. Box
NEW KOFORIDUA ASH. REGION

A FAIR DEAL

As thousands more people discover Divine Chocolate every year, the cooperative's secure Fairtrade income continues to grow. Kuapa Kokoo is now a thriving democratic organisation with 45,000 members producing up to 1% of the world's cocoa. The proportion of that sold at the Fairtrade price is still very small but even that has had a real impact. The members decide how the Fairtrade premium of $150 per tonne is invested in their community, providing local access to clean drinking water to thousands of people (not just farmers), improving health prospects, and freeing up women to learn new skills which bring in extra income, and children to spend more time in school. Kuapa has built and developed schools ensuring more children get a good primary education (and exam results keep getting better), and set up a mobile healthcare scheme – which can reach the very isolated villages. The reliability of the Fairtrade income has also meant Kuapa can attract loans and better establish itself as a sound business. As Kuapa Kokoo also co-owns Divine Chocolate Ltd, they can share in Divine's profits too. In 2006 The Body Shop made the inspired decision to donate all their shares in Divine to Kuapa Kokoo, and then in 2007 Divine Chocolate Inc was launched in the USA, also co-owned by Kuapa – so the benefits of farmer-ownership keep growing.

THE PERFECT INGREDIENT

Using the best ingredients to make Divine makes Divine in turn the perfect ingredient for cooking with chocolate... and here is the proof! More than one hundred delectable recipes exclusively created by chocolate expert Linda Collister, using Divine in almost all its many varieties, and sumptuously photographed by Lisa Barber. Illustrating this introduction is a collection of images from the lives of the Kuapa Kokoo farmers to whom this book is dedicated. Farmers from Kuapa Kokoo fly over to join us every year for Fairtrade Fortnight and are delighted by our love of chocolate, and judging from Mary Antwi Nyamekye and Comfort Kumeah's undisguised joy on tasting chocolate and cake for the first time in Bristol, these recipes would be an enormous hit with Kuapa too. We'll make sure every time we have Kuapa visitors we'll try a new recipe with them!

The unmistakable aroma of cooking and baking with chocolate is one of life's culinary pleasures – we hope the recipes here will introduce you to some new ideas and new twists on familiar favourites....

With every mouth-watering chooolate creation you make, if it's Divine it will not only be as good as its name, it will also mean that thousands of farmers can be sure of a fairer deal and a brighter future.

I hope you enjoy this book.

SOPHI TRANCHELL
MANAGING DIRECTOR,
DIVINE CHOCOLATE LTD

" Divine by name Divine by nature. The holistic ethic of Divine is one that many other chocolate manufacturers would do well to heed. Taking infinite care of its suppliers, the essential cocoa farmers whose lives are the better for it, provides a better cocoa bean, more time taken in harvesting, fermentation and drying and therefore better for us. Better for us because we are privileged to eat the result ie a mouthful of intense, very smooth, delectable chocolate knowing that we are all in a 'win-win' situation. Divine delivers what it promises."

Sara Jayne-Stanes,
Director of The Academy
for Culinary Arts and world-renowned chocolate expert

" For us, farmer ownership always made Divine Chocolate special. For the first time our members benefit as owners of a wonderful chocolate brand, and not only as suppliers of excellent fairly traded cocoa."

Mr Ohemeng Tinyase, Managing Director, Kuapa Kokoo Ltd

ADINKRA SYMBOLS

Divine Chocolate is adorned with traditional West African
Adinkra symbols. Each symbol has its own special meaning,
representing something integral to Ghanaian culture.
These symbols are still in use today serving to deliver
messages of goodwill. Divine chocolate is decorated with
a small selection of these symbols in celebration of our
relationship with Kuapa Kokoo and Ghana.

ADINKRAHENE
Charisma &
leadership

MMRA KRADO
Authority,
legitimacy

NKYINKIME
Balance in life

AKOMA
Patience and
harmony

NKRUMAKESE
Greatness, quality

DWENNIMMEN
Humility and
inner strength

OWIA KOKROKO
Vitality and
enlightenment

**ANANSE
NTONTAN**
Wisdom, creativity

DENKYEM
Adaptability

OWIA AHOCDEN
Life giving

SANKOFA
Revival

ASASE YE DURU
Sanctity of
mother earth

**BOA ME NA
MMOA WO**
Interpendence

MATE MASIE
Wisdom and
knowledge

DUA AFE
Life, beauty

SANKOFA
Learning from
the past

MPATAP
Reconciliation,
peace

KOKROBOTIE
Co-operation

AYA
Endurance,
perserverance

FI-HANKRA
Family and
solidarity

**FUNTUNFUNEFU-
DENKYEMFUNEFU**
Democracy,
shared destiny

BEFORE WE BEGIN...
(A FEW TIPS)

Here are just a few pointers to get you started and steer you clear of trouble.

STORING CHOCOLATE

Always wrap well and store in a cool, dry place away from other foods. Don't store in the fridge, or anywhere that the temperature is likely to drop below 13C, as beads of moisture will form as it comes back to room temperature. Working with chocolate in hot, humid weather or in a steamy kitchen can be tricky, so try to work when it's cool.

CHOPPING CHOCOLATE

Always use a clean, dry chopping board and a large sharp knife for chopping up chocolate. You can also use a food processor, just make sure you use the 'pulse' button in short bursts to avoid overworking the chocolate and turning it into a sticky mess. If you are going on to melt the chocolate, make sure it is cut or broken into even-sized pieces so it melts evenly. Before you try to chop or grate chocolate in hot weather chill it for a few minutes, just until firm.

MELTING CHOCOLATE

Never believe a cook who tells you that they have never had a problem melting chocolate. Melting chocolate is not foolproof and everyone gets it wrong sometimes because chocolate melts at a very low temperature (30C) – think about that ability to 'melt-in-the mouth' – it also tends to 'seize' and burn when over-heated (above 44C). Milk chocolate and white chocolate melt at a lower temperature than dark chocolate so even more care must be taken. But it's not difficult, as long as you pay attention and don't answer the phone or wander off for a coffee!

Start by breaking the chocolate, or chopping it with a large sharp knife or in the food processor, into even-sized pieces so it melts at an even rate. Put the chocolate into a heatproof bowl and set over a pan of steaming not boiling water. The water must not touch the base of the bowl or start to boil. Don't let any of the hot water or steam come into contact with the melting chocolate. If the recipe says to add liquid (coffee, a liqueur, cream, water) add it to the bowl with the chocolate before you set it over the pan of water.

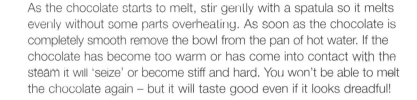

As the chocolate starts to melt, stir gently with a spatula so it melts evenly without some parts overheating. As soon as the chocolate is completely smooth remove the bowl from the pan of hot water. If the chocolate has become too warm or has come into contact with the steam it will 'seize' or become stiff and hard. You won't be able to melt the chocolate again – but it will taste good even if it looks dreadful!

MICROWAVING

You can melt chocolate in the microwave, but take great care! Make sure it is completely dry inside before you start and use a dry bowl. Consult the handbook first but if in doubt use the lowest setting and check the progress every 10 seconds to be on the safe side. Remember that milk and white chocolate need less time than dark, (along with adding butter or a liquid to the chocolate).

PIPED DECORATIONS

These look impressive on a cake, tart or mousse and are quite easy to make. Pour smooth melted chocolate (dark, milk or white) into a greaseproof paper icing bag. Leave to cool for a couple of minutes so the chocolate is slightly less runny then snip off the end of the bag.

Draw the outline of a shape or letter on non-stick baking paper or wax paper, turn the paper over (so the pencil mark is underneath) then pipe chocolate over the outline. Leave to set then peel away the paper. You can also draw free-hand and swirl patterns or overlapping circles of chocolate. When set break into pieces or cut into neat discs with a warmed round biscuit cutter. To make curved shapes drape the paper over a rolling pin while the piped chocolate sets.

CHOCOLATE CUPS

To make small chocolate cups that can hold mousse or truffles or chocolate dipped nuts you need a clean muffin tin or tray. Turn the tin upside down and cover the underside with cling film, making sure the film is pressed down tightly between and around each mould. Pipe swirls of chocolate around the sides of each mould, with a more solid chocolate base, then pipe a circle of chocolate around the top edge to make a rim to hold the whole cup in place. Leave until firm then carefully lift the cups off the cling film.

CHOCOLATE WAVES

To make chocolate 'waves' spread melted chocolate onto strips of waxed paper or non-stick baking paper then drape the paper up and down over a line of rolling pins, glass jars or tin cans set slightly apart. Leave to set then peel the chocolate off the paper and break into 'waves' to decorate the top or sides of a large cake. This looks very good done in two or three colours (let one chocolate set before adding another colour of chocolate).

CHOCOLATE SHAVINGS

These are wonderfully useful for covering the top and sides of cakes, as well as for decorating little cakes, tarts, mousses, trifles and ice-cream. Line a shallow tin with non-stick baking paper or wax paper, then hold a bar of chocolate with a sheet of kitchen paper and grate the chocolate into the tin using the large hole side of a grater. For best results the chocolate should be at room temperature. For curly 'wood shavings' peel the bar of chocolate with a vegetable peeler, and to get curved shavings, set the chocolate bar upside down in the lined tin. Hold it down firmly with a sheet of paper towel and scrape with a melon-ball cutter to make curved shavings.

CHOCOLATE BARK

Another very easy way to decorate recipes with chocolate is to add shards of 'bark'. Again, start by lining a baking tray with non-stick baking paper. Spread melted chocolate about 2mm thick over the paper and leave to set before breaking into shards. To make marbled bark, spread melted white or milk chocolate over dark chocolate just as it is beginning to set, then quickly marble the two colours with a cocktail stick or the end of a teaspoon and leave to set completely before breaking into pieces.

ALMOND BARK

For a chunkier and less delicate decoration nut bark tastes and looks impressive, and is still simple to make. Use equal quantities of chocolate and nuts. Melt the chocolate and toast the almonds – they can be left whole or cut into 2 or 3 slivers. Mix the nuts into the melted chocolate then spread evenly (in a fairly thin layer) onto a baking tray lined with wax paper or non-stick baking paper. Leave to set completely, then break up into shards. You can also use other nuts, lightly toasted – walnut, pecans, macadamia, hazelnuts or pistachios – and dark, milk or white chocolate.

BISCUITS
& COOKIES

VERY FRENCH CHOCOLATE MACAROONS

Filled chocolate macaroons remind me of Paris and those elegant gilt and marbled salons de thé. They are best eaten the next day (if you can wait) as the chocolate becomes more intensely flavoured and the texture slightly gooey.

MAKES 8 FILLED MACAROONS

For the macaroons
100g bar Divine dark chocolate
150g ground almonds
150g caster sugar
1 tablespoon Divine cocoa
3 large free range egg whites

For the filling
100g bar Divine dark chocolate
100ml double cream
15g unsalted butter, at room temperature
1–2 baking trays lined with non-stick baking parchment

Heat the oven to 140C/275F/Gas 1.

Break up the chocolate, put it into a bowl and melt gently (see page 16). Put aside until needed. Put the ground almonds, sugar and cocoa into a bowl and mix thoroughly. Using an electric mixer or whisk, beat the egg whites until they form soft peaks. Gradually whisk in the cocoa mixture. Gently fold in the melted chocolate using a metal spoon – the meringue mixture will collapse.

Put a heaped tablespoon of the mixture onto the prepared tray and gently spread to a round about 7cm across. Repeat with the rest of mixture to form 16 rounds. Bake for an hour until firm. Leave to cool for a couple of minutes on the baking tray and when firm enough transfer to a wire rack to cool completely.

Meanwhile, make the filling: break up the bar of chocolate and put it into a heatproof bowl. Heat the cream until scalding hot but not boiling then pour over the chocolate. Leave for a minute then add the butter and stir gently until smooth. Leave until cool then beat well with a wooden spoon until thick and fluffy. Sandwich pairs of macaroons together with plenty of the mousse filling. Leave for at least an hour before eating – they're at their best the next day.

Store in an airtight container. Not suitable for freezing.

DOUBLE CHOCOLATE PRETZELS

These rather decorative biscuits are made from rich, buttery chocolate dough that's easy to make in a food processor. After baking, they are coated in melted dark chocolate and sprinkled with emerald green pistachios.

MAKES 20 PRETZELS

225g plain flour
2 tablespoons Divine cocoa
100g icing sugar
100g unsalted butter, straight
    from fridge, diced
1 large free range egg, beaten

To finish
100g bar Divine dark chocolate
15g unsalted butter, soft
2 tablespoons pistachio nuts,
    chopped
icing sugar for sprinkling

2 baking trays, greased

Set the oven at 180C/350F/Gas 4.

Put the flour, cocoa, icing sugar, diced butter, and beaten egg into the bowl of a food processor. Whiz for about a minute until the ingredients come together to make a ball of dough. Remove the dough from the processor and divide into 20 fairly equal portions. With your hands, roll each portion into a sausage about 20cm long, then shape into a pretzel, that is, make a circle, then twist the ends as if making a knot.

Arrange the pretzels slightly apart on the baking trays to allow for spreading. Bake in the heated oven for 10–12 minutes until firm but not coloured around the edges. Remove the trays from the oven and set on a cooling rack. Leave the pretzels to cool completely on the trays.

To make the chocolate coating, gently melt the chocolate (see page 16) and stir in the butter. Dip half of each pretzel into the chocolate, or use a round-bladed knife and spread the chocolate. Set on non-stick baking paper or wax paper and sprinkle with the chopped nuts, leave until set and firm. Sprinkle the non-coated side of each pretzel with icing sugar.

Store in an airtight container and eat within 4 days.

DIVINE   HEAVENLY CHOCOLATE RECIPES

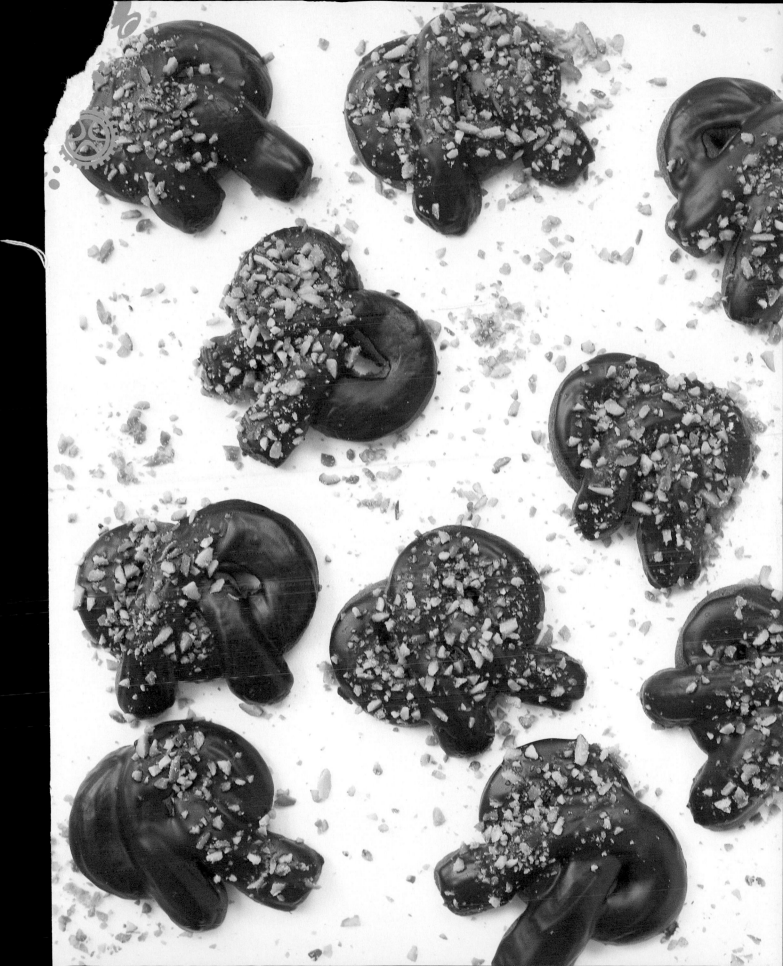

LAVA PEANUT COOKIES

My son Dan invented these easy and fun to make cookies for a cooking project at school – they even got an award! Don't overcook though, and choose top-quality sugar-free peanut butter for the best taste. The lava – an easy chocolate fudge icing – is added after baking.

MAKES 24 COOKIES

For the dough
115g unsalted butter, soft
100g smooth peanut butter
125g light muscovado sugar
1 large free range egg, lightly
   beaten
½ teaspoon vanilla essence
225g self-raising flour

For the lava
100g bar Divine dark chocolate
15g unsalted butter, very soft
2 tablespoons golden syrup

2 baking trays, greased

Heat the oven to 180C/350F/Gas 4.

Put the soft butter, peanut butter, sugar, beaten egg, vanilla and flour into a mixing bowl. Mix with a wooden spoon until thoroughly combined. Take walnut-sized portions of the dough, about a tablespoon, and roll into balls with your hands.

Arrange them on the baking trays, setting them slightly apart to allow for spreading. Press your thumb down into the centre of each ball to make a deep hollow. Bake in the heated oven for about 12 minutes until just golden. Remove the trays from the oven, set them on a cooling rack and leave to cool completely.

While the cookies are cooling make the lava filling. Gently melt the chocolate (see page 16) then stir in the soft butter and the golden syrup to make a smooth thick sauce. Using a teaspoon, carefully fill the hollow in each cookie with the chocolate lava and leave until set.

Store in an airtight container and eat as soon as possible, before the cookies soften.

TRY THIS TOO... EXTRA NUTTY COOKIES

After rolling the dough into balls, roll them in 100g of roasted, chopped, unsalted peanuts – coat evenly. Arrange on the baking trays and finish as above.

DIVINE DARK AND WHITE PINWHEEL BISCUITS

These cute biscuits, made from a shortbread mixture, are even richer than the usual recipes because they are made with both dark and white Divine chocolate.

MAKES 30 BISCUITS

$\frac{1}{2}$ x 45g bar Divine dark
   chocolate
$\frac{1}{2}$ x 45g bar Divine white
   chocolate
125g unsalted butter, very soft
100g caster sugar
1 large free range egg, beaten
1 teaspoon vanilla essence
250g plain flour
1 teaspoon baking powder
a good pinch of salt

several baking trays, greased

Break up the dark chocolate, put into a heatproof bowl and melt gently (see page 16). Remove the bowl from the heat and leave to cool until needed. Do the same with the white chocolate. Put the soft butter and sugar into the bowl of a food mixer and beat until light and fluffy. Gradually mix in the egg, followed by the vanilla, beating well.

Sift the flour, baking powder and salt into the bowl and gently mix in, using the lowest possible speed.

Remove half of the dough and mix into the cooled melted white chocolate. When thoroughly combined wrap in cling film and chill for 30 minutes until firm. Add the cooled melted dark chocolate to the remaining dough in the mixer bowl and combine thoroughly. Remove from the bowl, and wrap and chill as for the white chocolate mixture.

Set the piece of white chocolate dough between 2 sheets of cling film and roll out to a rectangle about 30 x 20 cm. Place the dough on a tray and return it to the fridge while you roll out the dark dough in the same way.

To assemble the pin wheels set the white chocolate rectangle on the work surface. Peel off the top sheet of cling film, then do the same for the dark dough and invert it onto the white dough. Peel off the uppermost sheet of cling film then roll up the two rectangles of dough – like a Swiss roll – starting from one long side to make a long thin roll. Cover and chill for 20 minutes.

Meanwhile, heat the oven to 180C/350F/Gas 4. Cut the roll into even-sized slices 1cm thick and set slightly apart on the prepared trays. Bake in the heated oven for 10–12 minutes until firm and barely coloured. Leave to cool for a couple of minutes and then transfer to a wire cooling rack and leave to cool completely.

Store in an airtight container and eat within 5 days.

THE ULTIMATE CHOC CHIP COOKIES

Rather than using the usual supermarket chocolate drops, these cookies are made with proper chunks of lovely dark chocolate, plus extra cocoa and crunchy nuts.

MAKES 18 LARGE COOKIES

1 x 100g bar Divine dark chocolate
100g walnut or pecan pieces
125g unsalted butter, soft
100g caster sugar
100g light muscovado sugar
1 large free range egg
220g plain flour
3 tablespoons Divine cocoa powder
½ teaspoon baking powder
½ teaspoon bicarbonate of soda

2 non-stick baking trays, ungreased

Heat the oven to 180C/350F/Gas 4.

Break up the chocolate into squares and mix with the nuts. Set aside until needed.

Put the soft butter and the sugars into the bowl of a food mixer and beat with the whisk attachment until soft and fluffy. Scrape down the sides then beat in the egg.

Remove the bowl from the mixer and sift the flour, cocoa, baking powder and bicarbonate of soda into the bowl. Mix well then stir in the chocolate squares and nuts.

Using a heaped tablespoon of mixture for each cookie, roll the mixture into balls then arrange them on the baking trays, flatten slightly with your fingers, spacing the cookies well apart to allow for spreading. Bake in the heated oven for about 12–15 minutes or until just firm, and then remove the trays from the oven and leave to cool for 5 minutes before transferring the cookies to a wire rack to cool completely.

Store in an airtight container and eat within 5 days or freeze for up to a month.

WHITE CHOCOLATE COOKIES STUDDED WITH CRANBERRIES

Dried cranberries (you could also use dried cherries) with their slight sharpness and brilliant colour are excellent combined with really good white chocolate.

MAKES 20 COOKIES

1 x 100g bar Divine white chocolate
125g unsalted butter, very soft
125g light muscovado sugar
1 large free range egg
1 teaspoon vanilla essence
150g plain flour
$\frac{1}{2}$ teaspoon baking powder
a good pinch of salt
50g dried cherries or cranberries

2 baking trays lined with non-stick baking parchment

Heat the oven to 180C/350F/Gas 4.

Break up or chop the chocolate into pieces about the size of your little finger nail. Set aside until needed. Put the soft butter, sugar, egg, vanilla, flour, baking powder and salt into the bowl of a food mixer. Beat until thoroughly combined, scraping down the bowl once or twice. Stir in the chocolate pieces and the dried fruit.

Take a heaped teaspoon of the mixture and put it onto the prepared tray, using another teaspoon to push the mixture off the spoon and into a rough mound. Repeat with the rest of the mixture, spacing the mounds well apart to allow for spreading. Bake in the heated oven for about 15 minutes until a light golden brown. Remove the trays from the oven, leave to cool for a minute then carefully transfer the cookies to a wire rack and leave to cool completely.

Store in an airtight container and eat within 4 days or freeze for up to a month.

DIVINE   HEAVENLY CHOCOLATE RECIPES

AUSTRALIAN CHUNKY DARK AND WHITE COOKIES

A rich but not too sweet combination of dark chocolate cookie dough studded with good-sized chunks of white chocolate and macadamia nuts. It's important to use a freshly opened pack of nuts, when they are at their best – tasty and crunchy.

MAKES ABOUT 18 COOKIES

125g unsalted butter, softened
75g light muscovado sugar
75g caster sugar
1 large free range egg, beaten
½ teaspoon vanilla essence
150g plain flour
30g Divine cocoa powder
½ teaspoon bicarbonate of soda
a good pinch of salt
1 x 100g bar Divine white chocolate
50g macadamia nuts

several baking trays, greased

Heat the oven to 180C/350F/Gas 4.

Put the soft butter and the sugars into the bowl of a food mixer and beat until soft and creamy. Beat in the egg and vanilla (you could also use a mixing bowl and wooden spoon). Sift the flour, cocoa, bicarbonate of soda and salt into the bowl and stir in, mixing well to combine all the ingredients.

Break up the chocolate into squares then cut or break each square in half. If necessary, chop the nuts in half. Add the chocolate and nuts to the bowl and work in. Using about a tablespoon of mixture for each cookie, drop the mixture onto the prepared trays, spacing the cookies well apart to allow for spreading. Gently flatten each cookie slightly so the mixture cooks evenly then bake in the heated oven for 12–15 minutes until just firm. Remove the trays from the oven, leave to cool for a couple of minutes then carefully transfer the cookies to a wire rack and leave to cool completely.

Store in an airtight container and eat within 4 days.

INCREDIBLY RICH FUDGE AND NUT SHORTBREAD

If you like Millionaire's Shortbread you should really taste these – the nutty almond topping is a good contrast to the texture of the sticky fudge filling, made by heating condensed milk with butter and sugar until you get a luxurious caramel.

MAKES 16 SQUARES

For the shortbread base
250g plain flour
a good pinch each grated
   nutmeg and ground cinnamon
75g caster sugar
175g unsalted butter, chilled and
   diced

For the fudge layer
75g unsalted butter
75g caster sugar
397g can condensed milk

For the nut topping
100g bar Divine dark chocolate
15g unsalted butter, very soft
50g toasted almonds, roughly
   chopped

20cm square tin, about 5cm
   deep, greased

Heat the oven to 180C/350F/Gas 4.

Put all the ingredients for the base into the bowl of a food processor and whiz until pea-sized lumps of dough form. Tip the mixture into the prepared tin and spread evenly, then lightly flour your fingers and press onto the base of the tin. Prick all over with a fork and then bake in a heated oven for 20–25 minutes until a pale golden colour. Remove from the oven and leave to cool completely.

When the base is cold make the filling: melt the butter with the sugar in a heavy non-stick saucepan. Stir in the condensed milk and gently bring the mixture to the boil, stirring constantly. Boil, stirring constantly for 5 minutes until the mixture turns a light caramel colour. Pour the boiling caramel over the base and leave to set.

To finish, gently melt the chocolate (see page 16), then stir in the butter and toasted nuts. Spread evenly over the fudge layer and leave to set. Cut into squares with a sharp knife.

Store in an airtight container and eat within 4 days. Not suitable for freezing.

LUXURIOUS FLAPJACKS

Flapjacks are both comforting and a treat, ideal for a long journey or picnic with a flask of coffee or hot chocolate. I love the combination of dark chocolate and whole almonds – here, the chocolate melts into the oats in great splodges. Use your favourite honey, I like orange blossom for this recipe.

CUTS INTO
36 PIECES

100g unsalted butter
130g clear orange blossom
*   honey*
2 tablespoons light muscovado
*   sugar*
300g porridge oats
2 tablespoons self-raising flour
100g blanched almonds
1 x 100g bar Divine dark
*   chocolate, broken into squares*

20.5 x 28cm brownie or traybake
*   tin, greased and base-lined*

Heat the oven to 160C/350F/Gas 3.

Put the butter, honey and sugar into a pan large enough to hold all the ingredients, and heat gently stirring frequently until the butter has melted. Remove the pan from the heat and stir in all the remaining ingredients. When thoroughly combined, tip the mixture into the prepared tin and spread evenly. Press the mixture into the tin with the back of a spoon then bake in the heated oven for 25 minutes until lightly golden. Remove from the oven and leave until completely cold before turning out and cutting or breaking into pieces.

Store in an airtight container and eat within 5 days.

REALLY QUICK AND EASY CHOCOLATE COOKIES

Even a complete novice could make these cookies; they really are so simple because everything is mixed in a saucepan then simply spooned out onto a tray and baked. I like walnuts but pecan pieces or chopped hazelnuts would be just as good.

MAKES 24 COOKIES

1 x 45g bar Divine dark or milk
   chocolate
50g walnut pieces
125g unsalted butter
100g dark muscovado sugar
100g caster sugar
1 large free range egg, lightly
   beaten
150g porridge oats
125g plain flour
$1/4$ teaspoon bicarbonate of soda
$1/2$ teaspoon vanilla essence

several baking trays, lightly
   greased

Set the oven at 180C/350F/Gas 4.

Chop the chocolate into small pieces – about the size of your little fingernail. Mix with the walnut pieces and set aside until needed. Put the butter into a medium pan and melt gently. Remove the pan from the heat and stir in the sugars using a wooden spoon. When thoroughly mixed, beat in the egg. Add the oats and mix in, followed by the flour, bicarbonate of soda and the vanilla essence. Add the chocolate and nuts and mix thoroughly.

Scoop the mixture onto the trays, using a tablespoon of mixture for each cookie, spacing them well apart to allow for expansion. Bake in the heated oven for about 15 minutes until lightly browned. Cool the biscuits on the trays for a minute then transfer to a wire rack and leave to cool completely.

Store in an airtight container and eat within a week.

TOASTED PECAN SHORTBREADS

Pecans and chocolate work beautifully together, the flavours being more than the sum of their parts. Toasting the nuts intensifies their flavour, but watch carefully to avoid scorching. Use a bag of freshly opened nuts if possible as once opened they quickly lose their taste.

MAKES 24 SHORTBREADS

150g pecan nuts
3 tablespoons Divine cocoa powder
200g unsalted butter, very soft
100g caster sugar
300g plain flour
a good pinch of salt
icing sugar for sprinkling

several baking trays, greased

Heat the oven to 180C/350F/Gas 4.

Put the nuts into an ovenproof dish and toast in the heated oven for about 10 minutes until lightly coloured. Remove from the oven and leave to cool completely. Tip the nuts into the bowl of a food processor, add the cocoa and run the machine to make a fairly fine powder. Set aside until needed.

Put the soft butter and sugar into a mixing bowl and beat well with a wooden spoon. Work in the flour and salt to make rough looking dough then add the nut mixture and briefly stir in. Using your hands, work the mixture until it comes together to make a fairly stiff dough.

Turn out onto a lightly floured work surface and shape into a log about 18cm long and 7cm wide. Using a large sharp knife cut the log into 24 slices. Set slightly apart on the prepared baking trays (if the slices fall apart as you are transferring them then just press them back together).

Bake for 10–12 minutes until just firm. Remove the trays from the oven, dust the shortbreads with icing sugar then leave to cool completely before lifting them off.

Store in an airtight container and eat within 4 days.

The dough can be shaped into a log then wrapped tightly and kept in the fridge for up to 5 days before baking.

BROWNIES

IVINE BROWNIES

No nuts, no coffee, nothing added to these brownies to distract from the main attraction – dark chocolate and cocoa. Take care not to overcook, brownies are meant to be gooey in the middle – it's what makes them so gorgeous to eat!

MAKES 24 PIECES

2 x 100g bars Divine dark chocolate
100g unsalted butter, very soft
250g caster sugar
4 large free range eggs, beaten to mix
1 teaspoon vanilla essence
60g plain flour
60g Divine cocoa powder

20.5 x 25.5cm brownie tin or baking tin greased and base-lined

Heat the oven to 180C/350F/Gas 4.

Break up the dark chocolate. Put into a heatproof bowl and melt gently (see page 16).

Remove the bowl from the heat and leave to cool until needed. Put the butter and sugar into the bowl of a food mixer and beat until fluffy. Gradually beat in the eggs, beating well after each addition. Beat in the vanilla essence. Spoon the cooled melted chocolate onto the mixture then mix in thoroughly. Sift the flour and cocoa onto the mixture and gently stir in. When completely combined spoon the mixture into the prepared tin and spread evenly.

Bake in the heated oven for about 20 minutes until firm to the touch but still a bit fudgy – the chocolate will continue to cook slightly for a few minutes after coming out of the oven. Remove the tin from the oven and set on a wire cooling rack. Leave to cool completely before cutting into pieces. Delicious eaten warm with ice-cream.

Store in an airtight container and eat within 4 days.

AFTER-DINNER BROWNIES

A simple but rich brownie, made with melted dark chocolate and a layer of Divine After Dinner Mints. Cut into small squares and serve with coffee. A rather elegant and grown-up treat.

CUTS INTO 20 PIECES

1 x 100g bar Divine dark chocolate
100g unsalted butter, diced
3 large free range eggs
200g caster sugar
100g plain flour
3 tablespoons Divine cocoa powder
1 x 200g box Divine After Dinner Mints

20.5cm x 25.5cm brownie tin or cake tin, well-greased

Heat the oven to 180C/350F/Gas 4.

Break up the dark chocolate, put into a heatproof bowl with the butter and melt gently (see page 16). Remove the bowl from the heat and cool until needed.

Break the eggs into the bowl of a food mixer and add the sugar and beat, using the whisk attachment, until very thick and frothy. Whisk in the melted chocolate mixture. Sift the flour and cocoa into the bowl and gently stir in. Spoon about half the mixture into the prepared tin and spread evenly. Arrange the Divine After Dinner Mints on top, in four rows of five mints, then top with the rest of the brownie mixture and spread evenly to cover the mints.

Bake in the heated oven for 25 minutes then remove the tin from the oven and set on a wire cooling rack. Run a round-bladed knife around the inside of the tin just to loosen the brownie and leave to cool completely before cutting into squares.

Store in an airtight container and eat within 5 days.

TOASTED HAZELNUT BROWNIES

Toasting the hazelnuts very gently increases their flavour as well as making them crunchier. The nuts are mixed with chunks of hazelnut milk chocolate and stirred into a dark chocolate brownie mixture. Very rich indeed!

MAKES 24 PIECES

100g blanched hazelnuts
1 x 100g bar Divine hazelnut chocolate
2 x 100g bars Divine dark chocolate
250g unsalted butter, diced
6 large free range eggs
350g caster sugar
150g plain flour
a pinch of salt

20.5 x 25cm brownie tin or cake tin, greased and base-lined

Heat the oven to 180C/350F/Gas 4.

Put the hazelnuts into an ovenproof dish and toast until lightly golden – about 7 minutes. Leave to cool. Break up the hazelnut chocolate into squares, add to the cooled nuts and set aside until needed.

Break up the dark chocolate and put it into a heatproof mixing bowl large enough to hold all the ingredients, add the butter then melt gently (see page 16). Remove the bowl from the heat and stir gently, leave to cool until needed. Put the eggs and sugar into another bowl and beat gently with a wooden spoon until just combined. Stir into the chocolate mixture followed by the flour and the salt. When thoroughly combined stir in the hazelnuts and the hazelnut chocolate. Pour into the prepared tin and spread evenly.

Bake for 30–35 minutes until a cocktail stick or skewer inserted halfway between the sides and the middle of the brownie comes out clean, and the mixture is still moist in the centre – it's important to not overcook them. Remove the tin from the oven, set on a wire rack and leave to cool completely before removing from the tin and cutting into pieces.

Store in an airtight container and eat within 5 days.

WALNUT FUDGE BROWNIES

These dense, wonderfully nutty, dark chocolate brownies are baked with an extra topping of sticky fudge and nuts – perfect eaten warm from the oven with ice-cream.

MAKES 24 PIECES

*1 x 100g bar Divine dark
  chocolate
125g unsalted butter, softened
250g caster sugar
1 teaspoon vanilla essence
2 large free range eggs, beaten
85g plain flour
2 tablespoons Divine cocoa
  powder
75g walnut pieces*

For the topping
*100g unsalted butter, softened
100g light muscovado sugar
2 tablespoons double cream
75g walnut pieces*

*20.5 x 25.5 cm brownie tin or
  baking tin, greased and base-
  lined*

Heat the oven to 180C/350F/Gas 4.

Break up the chocolate, put it into a heatproof bowl and melt gently (see page 16). Remove the bowl from the heat and leave to cool until needed. Put the butter into the bowl of a food mixer. Using the whisk attachment beat for a couple of minutes until the butter looks creamy then add the sugar, vanilla essence and eggs and beat well until thoroughly combined. Beat in the cooled melted chocolate. Sift the flour and cocoa powder onto the mixture and gently stir in. Add the nuts and mix thoroughly. Spoon the mixture into the prepared tin and spread evenly.

Bake in the heated oven for 30 minutes. While the brownie mixture is cooking, make the topping: beat the butter and sugar until thoroughly combined then beat in the cream. Stir in the nuts. At the end of the baking time remove the brownie mixture from the oven, but leave the oven turned on. Dot the topping mixture evenly over the top of the hot brownie mixture then return the tin to the oven and bake for a further 5–7 minutes until the topping is just turning colour and bubbling. Remove the tin from the oven and run a round-bladed knife inside the tin to loosen the brownie mixture then leave to cool before cutting into pieces.

Store in an airtight container and eat within 5 days.

BUTTERSCOTCH SWIRL BROWNIES

Slightly different from the usual brownie – the dark chocolate and nuts are added to the batter when it is in the tin to form large pools of melted chocolate. I've used pecans – the classic brownie ingredient – but you could add walnuts, hazelnuts, macadamia or even chopped Brazils for a change. Excellent with ice-cream and fudge sauce.

CUTS INTO 16

1 x 100g bar Divine dark
   chocolate
150g unsalted butter, very soft
225g light muscovado sugar
1 teaspoon vanilla essence
2 large free range eggs
175g plain flour
1 teaspoon baking powder
100g pecans

20.5cm square tin, well greased

Heat the oven to 180C/350F/Gas 4.

Break up the chocolate, put into a heatproof bowl and melt gently (see page 16). Remove the bowl from the heat and leave to cool until needed. Put the butter and sugar into the bowl of a food mixer and beat until creamy. Beat in the vanilla then beat in the eggs, one at a time, beating well after each addition.

Sift the flour and baking powder into the bowl and stir in. When thoroughly combined transfer the mixture to the tin and spread evenly. Scatter the pecans over the top then drizzle the melted chocolate over them. Using a round-bladed knife, swirl the chocolate and nuts through the cake mixture, to give a rough marbled effect.

Bake in the heated oven for about 25 minutes until just firm. Remove the tin from the oven, run a round-bladed knife around the inside of the tin to loosen the brownie and leave to cool on a wire rack.

Cut into pieces and store in an airtight container. Best eaten within 4 days.

THE MOST INCREDIBLY RICH BROWNIES

Dark chocolate walnut brownies with a baked cream cheese and walnut topping – almost a combination of brownie and cheesecake. Saved from going 'over-the-top' by the slight saltiness of really good cream cheese, plus wonderful chocolate! Very popular at parties.

CUTS INTO 24 PIECES

For the brownie mix

1 x 100g bar Divine dark chocolate
200g unsalted butter, diced
2 large free range eggs, at room temperature
375g caster sugar
250g plain flour
3 tablespoons Divine cocoa powder
$^3/_4$ teaspoon bicarbonate of soda
a good pinch of salt
1 teaspoon vanilla essence
50g walnut pieces

For the topping

100g unsalted butter, at room temperature
200g good quality cream cheese, at room temperature
$^1/_2$ teaspoon vanilla essence
1 large free range egg
200g icing sugar, sifted
50g walnut pieces

20.5 x 25.5cm brownie tin or baking tin, greased and base-lined

Heat the oven to 170C/325F/Gas 3.

Break up the chocolate and put into a heatproof bowl with the butter. Melt gently (see page 16), then remove the bowl from the heat and leave to cool until needed. Put the eggs into the bowl of a food mixer. Whisk until just combined then add the sugar and whisk until very thick and foamy. Sift the flour, cocoa, bicarbonate of soda and salt onto the mixture and gently fold in. Stir in the melted chocolate and the vanilla. Transfer the mixture to the prepared tin and spread evenly. Scatter over the nuts.

To make the topping: beat the butter with the cream cheese and vanilla until smooth and creamy, using a food mixer or bowl and wooden spoon. Beat in the egg followed by the icing sugar (if using a food mixer do this on low speed) to make a very smooth, thick batter.

Pour the topping over the brownie mixture and then gently spread it evenly. Scatter over the walnuts and bake in the heated oven for about 50 minutes until the topping is lightly coloured and the mixture is firm and set. Remove the tin from the oven and set on a wire cooling rack. Run a knife around the inside of the tin to loosen the brownie and then leave to cool before cutting into pieces.

Store in an airtight container in a cool place and eat within 3 days.

HALF COOKIE
HALF BROWNIE

Weird but wonderful – the mixture is pure brownie – lots of melted chocolate, plus nuts – but the mixture is shaped and baked like cookies (on a baking tray rather than in a tin). They are as good with ice-cream as with a cup of coffee.

MAKES ABOUT 20

2 x 100g bars Divine dark
   chocolate
50g unsalted butter, very soft
2 large free range eggs, at room
   temperature
150g caster sugar
25g plain flour
1 tablespoon Divine cocoa
$\frac{1}{4}$ teaspoon baking powder
a pinch of salt
100g walnut or pecan pieces
50g Divine chocolate (dark or
   flavoured), roughly chopped

2 baking trays lined with non-stick
   baking parchment

Heat the oven to 180C/350F/Gas 4.

Break up the two 100g bars of dark chocolate and melt gently (see page 16). Remove the bowl from the heat and stir in the butter. Leave to cool until needed. Put the eggs and sugar into the bowl of an electric mixer and whisk for 3–4 minutes until the mixture is very thick, pale and foamy. Whisk in the chocolate mixture. Sift the flour, cocoa, baking powder and salt onto the mixture. Add the nuts and chopped chocolate and gently mixed in.

Using a heaped tablespoon for each cookie, spoon the mixture onto the prepared trays, spacing the cookies well apart to allow for spreading. Bake in the heated oven for 10 minutes until just set and crazed with cracks. Remove the trays from the oven and leave on a wire rack until completely cold before gently removing.

Store in an airtight container and eat within 5 days.

WHITE CHOCOLATE BLONDIES WITH BLUEBERRIES AND MACADAMIA NUTS

The blondie batter is made with melted white chocolate for a really good taste, chunks of chocolate and nuts are mixed in for texture and fresh blueberries scattered on top act as a contrast to the sweet white chocolate.

CUTS INTO 24 PIECES

2 x 100g bars Divine white chocolate
200g unsalted butter, diced
3 large free range eggs, at room temperature
150g caster sugar
200g plain flour
1 teaspoon baking powder
50g macadamia nuts
150g fresh blueberries or fresh raspberries

20.5 x 25.5cm brownie tin or baking tin, greased and base-lined

Heat the oven to 180C/350F/Gas 4.

Break up one and a half bars of the chocolate (150g), put into a heatproof bowl with the diced butter and melt gently (see page 16), stirring frequently. Remove the bowl from the heat and leave to cool until needed.

Put the eggs into the bowl of a food mixer and whisk until frothy. Add the sugar and beat thoroughly until very thick and mousse-like. Whisk in the melted chocolate mixture. Sift the flour and baking powder onto the mixture and fold in with a large metal spoon. Roughly chop the remaining chocolate and the nuts and stir into the mixture.

Transfer to the prepared tin and spread evenly. Scatter over the berries then bake in the heated oven for about 25 minutes until golden and a skewer inserted into the blondie halfway between the sides and centre comes out clean. Remove the tin from the oven and set on a wire rack. Leave to cool completely before removing from the tin and cutting into pieces.

Store in an airtight container and eat within 3 days.

CAKES

HONEY CHOCOLATE MADELEINES

Use a good honey with a distinct, but not overwhelming, taste to balance the slight bitterness of the cocoa and almonds in these most elegant and light sponge cakes. Look out for special non-stick or flexible shell-shaped Madeleine moulds in cooks' shops and department stores.

MAKES 16

100g unsalted butter
2 large free range eggs, at room temperature
60g caster sugar
25g well-flavoured honey
75g plain flour
25g Divine cocoa powder
50g ground almonds
icing sugar for dusting

Madeleine moulds, brushed twice with melted butter

Heat the oven to 190C/375F/Gas5.

Melt the butter then leave to cool. Put the eggs into the bowl of a food mixer, whisk for a few seconds until mixed, then add the sugar and honey and whisk for 3–4 minutes until the mixture is very thick and light and the whisk leaves a distinct ribbon-like trail when lifted out of the bowl.

Sift the flour and cocoa into the bowl and briefly fold in with a large metal spoon. Add the almonds and fold in, finally pour in the melted butter and mix in. Spoon the mixture into the prepared moulds so each is about three-quarters full.

Bake in the heated oven for about 10 minutes or until the sponge can keep its shape when gently pressed. Watch the madeleines carefully as both honey and cocoa can easily scorch. Turn out onto a wire rack and leave to cool completely. Serve dusted with icing sugar.

Store in an airtight container and eat within 5 days.

DIVINE HEAVENLY CHOCOLATE RECIPES

FUDGY CHOCOLATE BARS

Slightly soft, sticky and rich with dark chocolate, these easy to make bars are good with a cup of coffee or eaten warm with ice-cream for dessert.

CUTS INTO 15

2 x 100g bars Divine dark
    chocolate
250g unsalted butter, diced
4 large free range eggs, at room
    temperature
250g light muscovado sugar
1 teaspoon vanilla essence
125g plain flour

23cm square cake tin, greased
    and base-lined

Heat the oven to 170C/325F/Gas3.

Break up the chocolate, put into a heatproof bowl with the butter and melt gently, stirring occasionally. Remove the bowl from the heat and leave to cool until needed.

Put the eggs, sugar and vanilla into the bowl of a food mixer. Using the whisk attachment beat until very thick and foamy about 3–4 minutes.

Using a large metal spoon, carefully fold in the melted chocolate mixture. Sift the flour onto the mixture and gently combine. Transfer the mixture into the prepared tin and spread evenly. Bake in the heated oven for 30 minutes or until a skewer inserted into the cake, halfway between the sides and the centre, comes out clean – the centre will be slightly soft.

Remove the tin from the oven and set on a wire rack. Run a round-bladed knife around the inside of the tin to loosen the cake then cut into bars. Leave to cool completely before removing from the tin.

Store in an airtight container and eat within 5 days.

REALLY RICH CUP CAKES

If you've never tried genuine cup cakes before, these are irresistible and sure to impress. The richness comes from all the dark chocolate; the soft moist crumb from the sour cream. You can leave them plainly iced or go crazy with sugar flowers, specks of gold leaf, white and dark chocolate shavings, fresh berries....

MAKES 12

For the cake mixture
2 x 100g bars Divine dark
  chocolate
200g unsalted butter, very soft
200g caster sugar
4 large free range eggs, at room
  temperature
100ml sour cream
200g self-raising flour

For the topping
1 x 100g bar Divine dark
  chocolate
1 tablespoon golden syrup
25g unsalted butter

12-hole muffin tray lined with
  paper muffin cases

TRY THIS TOO...

Heat the oven to 180C/350F/Gas 4.

Break up the chocolate bars and melt gently (see page 16). Remove the bowl from the heat and leave to cool until needed. Put the butter and sugar into the bowl of a food mixer and beat until light and creamy. Beat in the eggs one at a time, beating well after each addition.

Stir in the cream on low speed, followed by the flour and finally the melted chocolate, mixing gently until thoroughly combined. Spoon the mixture into the muffin cases so they are evenly filled then bake in the heated oven for about 25 minutes until firm to the touch. Remove the muffins from the tin and leave to cool on a wire rack.

Meanwhile, make the topping: break up the chocolate and melt gently. Remove the bowl from the heat and stir in the syrup and butter. Leave to cool and thicken slightly then either dip the top of the cup cakes into the topping or spoon it on. Leave to set.

Store in an airtight container and eat within 4 days. The un-iced cakes can be frozen for up to a month.

REALLY RICH LOAF CAKE

Make up the cup cake mixture as above and then spoon it into a 900g loaf tin (greased and base-lined). Bake in the oven heated to 180C/350F/Gas 4 for about 1 hour until a skewer inserted into the centre comes out clean. Cool for 5 minutes then remove the cake from the tin and leave to cool on a wire rack. Spread the topping thickly over the cake.

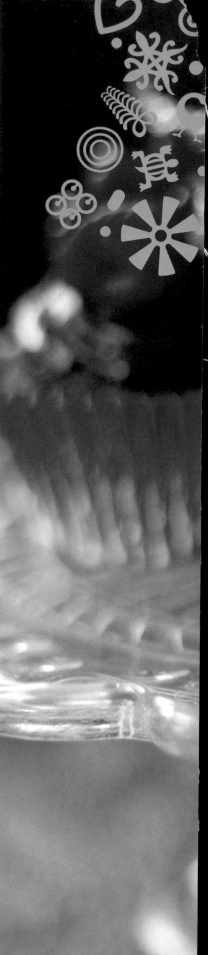

HEART OF HAZELNUT CHOCOLATE MUFFINS

These really light but intensely nutty muffins have hazelnuts both in the mixture and have a centre of Divine hazelnut milk chocolate. For a slightly less nutty, but equally delicious muffin, you could use a bar of Divine dark chocolate or Divine white for the centre instead.

MAKES 12 NOT-TOO-BIG MUFFINS

150g blanched hazelnuts
125g unsalted butter
4 large free range egg whites
100g plain flour
4 tablespoons Divine cocoa powder
3 tablespoons light muscovado sugar
150g icing sugar
1 x 100g bar Divine hazelnut milk chocolate
icing sugar for dusting

12-hole muffin tray lined with paper muffin cases

Heat the oven to 200C/400F/Gas 6.

Put the hazelnuts into a heatproof dish and toast in the heated oven for 5 minutes until golden. Remove and leave to cool completely then tip into the bowl of a food processor and grind to make a coarse powder. Set aside until needed.

Melt the butter and leave to cool. Put the egg whites into the bowl of a food mixer and whip until soft peaks form. Sift the flour, cocoa, muscovado and icing sugars onto the whites. Add the ground nuts and drizzle over the cooled melted butter. Using a large metal spoon gently fold all the ingredients together until just mixed. Break up the chocolate into 24 squares.

Spoon half of the mixture into the 12 muffin cases, giving each an equal amount. Add 2 squares of the chocolate to the middle of each and then cover with the rest of the muffin mixture.

Bake in the heated oven for 15–18 minutes until firm to the touch. Turn out of the tin onto a wire cooling rack and leave to cool. Dust with icing sugar before serving.

Best eaten the same day.

PAINS AU CHOCOLAT

If you are looking for a challenge, then try making your own Pains au Chocolat, the original, and best, after-school treat for generations of French school children. There are various stages involved to allow for chilling and rising times so it's best to start a day before you plan to eat them. Basically, its croissant dough – a combination of bread dough and puff pastry – wrapped around squares of dark chocolate, buttery, flaky and utterly delicious!

MAKES 12

3 tablespoons caster sugar
1 tablespoon sea salt
4 tablespoons milk powder
325ml cool water
500g unbleached white bread
  flour
1 x 7g sachet easy-blend dried
  yeast
250g unsalted butter (preferably
  French), chilled
2 x 100g bars Divine dark
  chocolate
1 free range egg yolk beaten with
  1 tablespoon milk to glaze

You will need several baking trays

Add the sugar, salt and milk to the measured water and stir until completely dissolved.

Put the flour into the bowl of a food mixer, add the dried yeast and mix in using the dough hook or K beater. Add the milk liquid and beat at the lowest speed just until the ingredients are thoroughly combined to make a soft, sticky dough that comes away from the sides of the bowl – about 1 minute. Do not knead or overwork the dough at this point.

Cover the bowl with a lid or put it into a large plastic bag and leave in a warm spot until the dough doubles in size – about 30 minutes. Gently punch down the dough to deflate then re-cover and put into the fridge overnight or at least 6 hours to firm up. Next day take the block of butter out of the fridge and place it between 2 sheets of greaseproof paper and pound it with a rolling pin to flatten it. Re-shape into a brick shape and repeat the process a few times until the butter is cold and firm but pliable. Finally shape the butter into a square with sides of about 12cm.

Turn out the chilled dough onto a lightly floured work surface. Punch down to deflate then shape the dough into a ball. Cut a deep cross in the top of the ball. Roll out the dough using a floured rolling pin in four directions (making a quarter turn after each rolling) so the dough looks like a cross with a thick rough square of dough in the centre. Place the butter on top of the rough square of dough, then fold the dough over the butter, tucking in the edges and making sure the butter is completely enclosed so it doesn't ooze out during the rolling and folding processes. Lightly sprinkle the dough with flour then roll out the dough to a rectangle about 30 x 60cm. Turn the rectangle on its side so one long side is facing you. Fold the dough in thirds – fold over the right third of dough (so it covers the centre portion) then fold over the left third to make a 3-layer sandwich of dough. Use the rolling pin to seal the edges. Set the dough on a plate, cover tightly and chill for 30 minutes. Repeat the rolling, folding and chilling process twice more, turning the dough a quarter turn to the left each time you start to roll.

After the third chilling, roll out the dough to a rectangle about 0.5cm thick and 32 x 62 cm. Using a large sharp knife, trim off the edges to make a neat rectangle 30x 60cm. Cut the rectangle into 12 smaller rectangles each 10 x 15 cm. Break up the chocolate into 12 fingers of four squares. Arrange a finger of chocolate along one short end of each dough rectangle then roll up. Arrange the rolls, seam-side underneath, well apart on the baking trays. Lightly brush the rolls with the egg glaze then leave to rise in a warm, humid and draught-free spot until doubled in size – about an hour.

Meanwhile, preheat the oven to 230C/450F/Gas 8. Lightly brush the rolls with glaze once more then bake in the heated oven for 10 minutes then reduce the heat to 200C/400F/Gas 6. and bake for a further 8–10 minutes until a good golden brown and crisp. Remove from the tray and leave to cool on a wire rack.

Best eaten within 24 hours. If eating the next day, gently warm before eating – take care not to eat whilst hot as the chocolate will burn your mouth.

DELICIOUSLY DIFFERENT CHRISTMAS CAKE

Once a year a traditional homemade rich fruit cake, makes a great treat. This is my favourite Christmas cake. It is flavoured with plenty of rum, and studded with squares of dark, bitter chocolate as a contrast to all the dried fruits. However, it goes against the norm by having the marzipan, not set on top of the finished cake as is traditional, but baked in the centre of the mixture, to give a deliciously moist and wonderfully flavoured special fruit cake. You can still add your favourite decorations or perhaps opt for Divine Chocolate Gold Coins or Divine Chocolate covered Apricots.

MAKES 1 LARGE CAKE

250g plain flour
2 teaspoons baking powder
a pinch of salt
50g ground almonds
175g unsalted butter, soft
175g light muscovado sugar
4 large free range eggs, at room temperature
4 tablespoons dark rum
300g mixed dried fruit and peel
100g whole blanched almonds, toasted and roughly chopped
2 x 100g bars Divine dark chocolate, broken into squares
250g readymade marzipan
2 tablespoons flaked almonds
icing sugar for dusting.

23cm round deep cake tin or springclip tin, greased and lined base and sides with greaseproof paper (or use a cake liner)

Heat the oven to 180C/350F/Gas 4.

Sift the flour with the baking powder and salt into a bowl. Stir in the ground almonds and set aside until needed. Put the soft butter and the sugar into the bowl of a food mixer, and using the whisk attachment beat until the mixture looks soft and creamy.

Break the eggs into another bowl and beat with a fork, just to break them up, and then gradually beat them into the butter mixture, beating well after each addition. Add a tablespoon of the flour mixture with each of the last 2 portions of egg to prevent the mixture from separating.

Remove the bowl from the mixer and add the rest of the flour mixture. Using a metal spoon, fold in the flour until almost combined and then add the rum and the mixed dry fruit and peel and stir in gently. Add the almonds and the chocolate squares and mix thoroughly. Spoon half of the cake mixture into the tin and spread evenly.

Knead the marzipan for a few seconds just to soften it then roll it out into a disc to fit into the tin. Set the disc on top of the cake mixture and press down gently to push out any air bubbles. Spoon the rest of the mixture on top and spread evenly. Make a shallow hollow in the centre, this will ensure the cake rises evenly. Sprinkle with the flaked almonds.

Bake in the heated oven for 30 minutes, and then reduce the oven temperature to 170C/325F/Gas 3 and bake for a further $1\frac{1}{4}$–$1\frac{1}{2}$ hours until golden and a skewer inserted into the centre of the cake down to the marzipan layer comes out clean. If it comes out a bit sticky, bake for another 5 minutes then test again (though it is hard to avoid both the marzipan and lumps of chocolate when testing).

Remove the cake from the oven and leave to cool completely on a wire cooling rack. Turn out, remove the lining paper, wrap in fresh paper and leave for 3–4 days before cutting. Dust with icing sugar just before serving.

Store in an airtight container. Best eaten within 3 weeks.

DIVINE   HEAVENLY CHOCOLATE RECIPES

RICH CHESTNUT AND CHOCOLATE CAKE

Around Christmas this type of cake is seen in the best cake shops in France, and especially Lyons; a wonderfully rich cake made from melted chocolate and pureed chestnuts, exquisitely decorated and topped with luxurious marrons glacés. It even looks impressive enough as a special birthday cake – serve small slices with whipped cream.

MAKES 1 LARGE CAKE

For the sponge
3 x 100g bars Divine dark chocolate
150g unsalted butter, diced
1 x 435g can unsweetened chestnut purée
5 large free range eggs, separated
1 teaspoon vanilla essence
50g plain flour
150g caster sugar

For the icing
1 x 100g bar Divine dark chocolate
25g unsalted butter, diced
1 tablespoon water
marrons glacés (candied chestnuts) to decorate

23cm springclip tin, greased and base-lined

Heat the oven to 180C/350F/Gas 4.

To make the sponge: break up the chocolate and put into a large heatproof bowl with the butter. Melt gently (see page 16) then remove the bowl from the heat. Break up the solid cylinder of chestnut purée with a fork then beat into the chocolate using a wooden spoon. Beat in the yolks and the vanilla. When the mixture is very smooth sift the flour into the bowl and stir in. Whisk the eggs whites until almost stiff then whisk in the caster sugar.

Using a large metal spoon work about a quarter of the whites into the chocolate mixture to loosen it then gently fold in the rest of the whites in three equal batches.

Spoon the mixture into the prepared tin and spread evenly. Bake in the heated oven for about 45 minutes or until a skewer inserted into the centre comes out just moist (rather than clean) but not sticky with mixture. Set the tin on a wire rack and run a round-bladed knife inside the tin to loosen the sponge then unclip and remove the cake from the tin. Leave on a wire rack to cool completely. The cake will sink and crack slightly.

To make the icing: break up the chocolate and put into a heatproof bowl. Add the diced butter and water and melt very, very gently without stirring (see page 16). Remove the bowl from the heat, stir once or twice until smooth. Invert the sponge onto a serving plate – it is easier to ice the flat base. Pour the icing over the cake and gently smooth it over the top and down the sides, using as few strokes as possible.

Leave until set then decorate with the marrons glacés. Store in an airtight container and eat within 4 days.

FIG, ALMOND AND CHOCOLATE CAKE FROM SOUTHERN FRANCE

This deceptively plain looking undecorated loaf cake actually tastes amazingly rich and complex! Use top quality soft-dried figs for the best results and speed things up by using a food processor to chop the chocolate and purée the figs.

MAKES 1 MEDIUM LOAF CAKE

200g soft-dried figs
200ml water
½ teaspoon bicarbonate of soda
100g unsalted butter, very soft
125g light muscovado sugar
2 large free range eggs, at room temperature, beaten to mix
100g ground almonds
100g self-raising flour
1 x 45g bar Divine dark chocolate, finely chopped or grated

450g loaf tin, greased and base-lined

Heat the oven to 180C/350F/Gas 4.

Using kitchen scissors snip the figs into quarters, discarding the stalks. Put into a pan with the water, bring to a boil then stir in the bicarbonate of soda and leave to cool.

Meanwhile, put the butter into the bowl of a food mixer and beat until creamy. Add the sugar and beat until light and fluffy. Gradually beat in the eggs, beating well after each addition. Stir in the almonds and the flour.

Tip the fig mixture into the bowl of a food processor and run the machine to make a coarse purée. Add to the cake mixture and mix in. When thoroughly combined stir in the finely chopped chocolate. Spoon the mixture into the prepared tin and spread evenly.

Bake in the heated oven for about 55 minutes or until a skewer inserted into the centre of the cake comes out clean. Set the tin on a wire rack and leave to cool completely before turning out.

Store in an airtight container and eat within 5 days.

ORANGE AND CHOCOLATE JACKSON POLLOCK CAKE

My son Dan named this cake after the abstract expressionist artist, Jackson Pollock – one of his favourites. It has a rectangular base of orange sponge topped with orange syrup and the topping is an artwork of dark chocolate drizzled and splashed on top (you could also add a drizzle of melted white chocolate too) – it's a really fun cake to make.

MAKES 1 CAKE

For the cake mixture
175g unsalted butter, very soft
175g caster sugar
3 large free range eggs
175g self-raising flour
2 unwaxed oranges

For the orange drizzle
75g caster sugar

For chocolate drizzle
1 x 100g bar Divine dark
    chocolate
15g unsalted butter

20.5 x 25cm brownie tin or 23cm
    springclip tin, greased and
    base-lined

Heat the oven to 180C/350F/Gas 4.

Put the soft butter, sugar, eggs and flour into the bowl of a food mixer. Wash the oranges and grate the zest with a fine grater or citrus zester. Add the zest to the bowl. Halve the oranges and squeeze out the juice – to make about 150ml. Spoon three tablespoons into the bowl and save the rest for the topping. Beat all the ingredients for the cake mixture until smooth and light. Spoon into the cake tin and spread evenly. Bake in the heated oven for 40–45 minutes or until a skewer inserted into the centre of the sponge comes out clean.

While the cake is baking make the orange drizzle: stir the sugar into the reserved orange juice. When the cake comes out of the oven set the tin on a wire cooling rack. Make deep holes in the cake with a skewer or cocktail stick then spoon over the orange mixture. Leave to cool completely then remove the cake from the tin.

To make the chocolate drizzle: break up the chocolate and melt gently (see page 16). Remove the bowl from the heat and stir in the butter. Then with a spoon, drizzle and splash the chocolate over the cake (see results overleaf), or – if you are of a more conservative nature! – spread it over instead. Leave to set.

Store in an airtight container and eat within 5 days.

OLD-FASHIONED CHOCOLATE BUTTERMILK POUND CAKE

A good, plain and simple cake made with cocoa powder for real flavour, plus buttermilk for lightness plus extra taste and a moist crumb. It doesn't need anything more than a simple shake of icing sugar to decorate and maybe a bowl of whipped cream to hand around.

MAKES 1 LARGE CAKE

200g plain flour
50g Divine cocoa powder
1 teaspoon baking powder
$\frac{1}{2}$ teaspoon bicarbonate of soda
a good pinch of salt
175g unsalted butter, softened
225g caster sugar
3 large free range eggs, separated
2 teaspoons instant coffee (powder or granules)
250ml buttermilk
icing sugar for dusting

23cm springclip tin, greased and base-lined

Heat the oven to 180C/350F/Gas 4.

Sift the flour with the cocoa, baking powder, bicarbonate of soda and salt three times onto a sheet of greaseproof paper. Set aside until needed.

Put the soft butter into the bowl of a food mixer. Using the whisk attachment beat for a minute until creamy then add three-quarters of the sugar and beat until very light and fluffy. Beat in the egg yolks one at a time, beating well after each addition.

Stir the coffee powder or granules into the buttermilk until dissolved. Fold the flour and buttermilk alternately in batches into the creamed mixture. Whisk the egg whites until soft peaks form then whisk in the remaining sugar. Fold the whites into the mixture in three batches. Spoon the mixture into the prepared tin and spread evenly.

Bake in the heated oven for 55–60 minutes or until a skewer inserted into the centre of the cake comes out clean. Set the tin on a wire rack and run a round-bladed knife around the inside of the tin to loosen the cake then unclip the tin. Leave until cold then serve dusted with icing sugar.

Store in an airtight container and eat within 5 days.

DEVIL'S FOOD CAKE

This is one of my favourite cakes yet not so easy to find these days. The sponge has to be very dark yet light and with a strong taste of chocolate. I couldn't choose between the white or dark filling and icing so I've included both so you can pick either a marshmallow frosting or a double chocolate fudge one. The cake tastes better and better after a day or so and keeps moist for several days.

MAKES 1 LARGE CAKE

For the sponge

1 x 100g bar Divine dark chocolate
175ml boiling water
4 tablespoons Divine cocoa
 powder
1 teaspoon bicarbonate of soda
125g unsalted butter, softened
175g light muscovado sugar
175g caster sugar
2 large free range eggs, at room
 temperature, beaten
1 teaspoon vanilla essence
300g plain flour
125ml sour cream, at room
 temperature

For the marshmallow frosting

350g caster sugar
2 large free range egg whites, at
 room temperature
a pinch of salt
1 tablespoon maple syrup
1 teaspoon vanilla essence
125ml water

Alternatively, for the fudge frosting

3 x 45g bars Divine dark chocolate
3 x 45g bars Divine milk
 chocolate
225ml sour cream

3 x 20.5cm sponge tins, greased
 and base-lined

Heat the oven to 180C/350F/Gas 4.

For the sponge: break up the chocolate, put into a heatproof bowl and melt gently (see page 16). Remove the bowl from the heat and leave to cool until needed. Pour the boiling water over the cocoa and mix or whisk well until smooth. Stir in the bicarbonate then stir into the melted chocolate. Put the butter into the bowl of a food mixer, add both sugars and whisk thoroughly until light. Gradually beat in the eggs, beating well after each addition. Beat in the vanilla. Mix in the flour alternately with the sour cream. When thoroughly combined stir in the chocolate mixture. Divide the sponge mixture equally between the three tins and spread evenly. Bake in the heated oven for 25–30 minutes until a skewer inserted into the centre of the cakes comes out clean. Turn out the cakes onto a wire rack and leave to cool completely.

To make the marshmallow frosting: put the caster sugar and the egg whites into a large heatproof mixing bowl. Set over a pan of gently simmering water and whisk using an electric whisk until just frothy. Add the salt, maple syrup and water and whisk on full speed for 7 minutes. Remove the bowl from the heat and continue whisking for another 15–20 minutes until the frosting has cooled and become very thick and white. Use immediately to sandwich and frost the top and sides of the cake. Leave for a couple of hours to set.

For the fudge icing: break up the bars of chocolate. Put into a heatproof bowl and melt gently (see page 16). Remove the bowl from the heat and stir gently then stir in the cream to make a smooth thick icing. Use to sandwich and cover the cake.

Store in an airtight container and eat within 5 days.

STICKY PEANUT BUTTER CAKE.

A traditional chocolate sponge cake but filled with an incredibly sticky combination of peanut butter and chocolate. Look out for top-quality peanut butter made without added sugar, and decorate with readymade peanut brittle or peanut crunch. For those who can't eat peanuts I've added some variations for fillings and toppings.

MAKES 1 LARGE CAKE

For the sponge
175g unsalted butter, softened
150g caster sugar
25g light muscovado sugar
3 large free range eggs, at room
    temperature
1 teaspoon vanilla essence
150g self-raising flour
30g Divine cocoa powder
2 tablespoons milk

For the filling
1 x 45g bar Divine dark chocolate
1 x 45g bar Divine milk chocolate
125g smooth peanut butter
25g unsalted butter, softened
2 teaspoons icing sugar, optional
2 teaspoons Divine cocoa
    powder, optional
peanut brittle to decorate

2 x 20.5cm sandwich tins,
    greased and base-lined

Heat the oven to 180C/350F/Gas 4.

To make the sponge: put the soft butter into the bowl of a food mixer and beat until creamy. Add both the sugars and beat until very light and fluffy. Gradually beat in the eggs, beating well after each addition. Beat in the vanilla. Sift the flour and cocoa powder into the bowl, add the milk and mix gently until thoroughly combined. Spoon the mixture equally into the prepared tins and spread evenly. Bake in the heated oven for 15–20 minutes, or until the sponge springs back when gently pressed and is starting to colour on top and has shrunk away from the sides of the tins. Turn out onto a wire rack. Remove the lining paper and leave to cool completely.

Meanwhile, make the filling and topping: break up both bars of chocolate and put into a heatproof bowl. Melt very gently (see page 16) then remove the bowl from the heat and leave to cool for a couple of minutes. Using a wooden spoon beat in the peanut butter and the soft butter. When very smooth taste the mixture – peanut butters vary in flavour from brand to brand so add a little icing sugar or cocoa powder as needed to give the taste you like.

Set one sponge layer on a serving plate. Spread with half the peanut filling. Cover with the second sponge then spread the rest of the peanut mixture on top. Decorate with shards of peanut brittle.

Store in an airtight container and eat within 5 days.

(Continued on page 74)

(Continued from page 72)

TRY THESE TOO...

OLD-FASHIONED CHOCOLATE SPONGE CAKE

Make the sponge following the recipe above, replacing the light muscovado sugar with more caster sugar making the total 175g of caster sugar. For the filling and topping: beat 125g soft unsalted butter with 400g sifted icing sugar, 3 tablespoons of sifted Divine cocoa powder and 3–4 tablespoons milk to make a smooth thick icing. For a mocha flavour replace the milk with cold strong coffee.

BLACK AND WHITE SPONGE CAKE

Make the sponge, using 175g soft unsalted butter, 175g caster sugar, a teaspoon vanilla essence, 175g self-raising flour, 3 eggs, 2 tablespoons milk. Instead of flavouring the sponge with cocoa (as above), mix in 1 x 45g bar Divine dark chocolate, finely chopped, before putting the mixture into the sponge tins. For the filling and topping: use the mixture given for the Old-fashioned Chocolate Sponge Cake (see above) omitting the cocoa and flavouring with a teaspoon of vanilla essence. Decorate the top with shavings of dark chocolate.

RED HOT CHILLI-PEPPER CHOCOLATE CAKE

Dried hot red chilli peppers work well with dark chocolate (see the Savoury section, pages 180–189, for more recipe ideas). Here the taste is intriguing rather than overwhelming – a cake with a kick rather than a punch. It is a flourless cake cooked very slowly in the oven in a water bath, helping make the texture soft and moist.

MAKES 1 MEDIUM CAKE

250g caster sugar
125ml water
2 dried red hot chilli peppers
3 x 100g bars Divine dark chocolate
4 tablespoons Divine cocoa powder
250g unsalted butter, at room temperature, diced
5 large free range eggs, at room temperature
3 tablespoons light muscovado sugar
icing sugar for dusting

23cm springclip tin, greased and base-lined, and the tin wrapped outside (base and sides) in a double layer of foil to seal the join, plus a roasting tin to act as a water bath.

Heat the oven to 180C/350F/Gas 4. Half fill the roasting tin with water and put it into the oven to heat up while you make the cake.

Put the sugar, water and chilli peppers into a medium pan and set over a very low heat, stirring occasionally until the sugar completely dissolves. Bring to the boil and boil rapidly for 10 seconds to make syrup. Remove the pan from the heat and leave to cool for 5 minutes.

Remove the chillies and discard. Break up the chocolate and stir it into the syrup with the cocoa. Once melted and smooth stir in the butter, a few pieces at a time. When completely smooth set aside until needed but don't allow the mixture to start to set.

Put the eggs and muscovado sugar into the bowl of a food mixer. Using the whisk attachment beat until very light and foamy. Stir in the warm chocolate mixture then transfer the cake batter to the prepared tin and spread evenly. Set the tin in the water bath in the oven and bake for 50 minutes. Remove the tin from the water bath and the oven and set on a wire cooling rack. Run a round-bladed knife around the inside of the tin to loosen the cake and leave to cool before unclipping. Dust with icing sugar and serve at room temperature or warm with whipped cream or crème fraîche.

Store in an airtight container and eat within 2 days.

AMERICAN PECAN AND CHOCOLATE 'COFFEE-CAKE'

This well-loved American 'Coffee Cake' doesn't actually contain any coffee but gets its name because it's traditionally served with a pot of coffee. Usually baked in a handsome elaborately decorated round Bundt (or funnel) tin its main ingredient is actually sour cream that gives it a wonderful moist texture and deep flavour. You could also make one tray of six individual cakes. Just follow the recipe and bake for 35 minutes.

MAKES 1 LARGE CAKE

For the streusel layers
100g pecan nuts
100g bar Divine dark chocolate
4 tablespoons light muscovado
  sugar
1 teaspoon ground cinnamon

For the cake mixture
250g unsalted butter, very soft
150g caster sugar
2 large free range eggs
250ml sour cream
300g plain flour
$\frac{1}{2}$ teaspoon bicarbonate of soda
2 teaspoons baking powder
a good pinch of salt
icing sugar for dusting

23cm Bundt tin, well-greased, or
  a 900g loaf tin, greased and
  base-lined

Heat the oven to 180C/350F/Gas 4.

For the streusel: put the pecans into a heatproof dish and toast in the heated oven for 10–15 minutes until just starting to colour. Remove and leave to cool completely.

Break up the chocolate and put into the bowl of a food processor and chop roughly. Add the cooled nuts, the muscovado sugar and the cinnamon and process until the nuts and chocolate are chopped to a medium-fine texture. Set aside until needed.

Put the soft butter into the bowl of a food mixer, and using the whisk attachment, beat until creamy. Beat in the sugar, and then when light and fluffy beat in the eggs one at a time, beating well after each addition. Finally, beat in the sour cream. Sift the flour, bicarbonate of soda, baking powder and salt into the bowl. Mix in gently with a large metal spoon. Spoon half the mixture into the prepared tin and spread evenly. Sprinkle half the streusel over the cake mixture. Gently spoon the rest of the cake mixture on top and spread evenly. Scatter the remaining streusel on the top and press the mixture gently down onto the cake batter with the back of a spoon. Bake in the heated oven for 45–55 minutes or until a skewer inserted in the centre comes out clean. Remove the tin from the oven and set on a wire rack. Leave to cool completely before turning out. Dust with icing sugar before serving.

Store in an airtight container and eat within 4 days.

SACHERTORTE

This legendary luxuriously rich chocolate sponge cake covered with a glossy layer of chocolate ganache (chocolate cream) was invented in 1832 by the chef at the Hotel Sacher in Vienna. Even today it remains extremely popular at the hotel where it is still made to the original recipe. It is the perfect cake or dessert for a special occasion.

MAKES 1 LARGE CAKE

For the sponge
2 x 100g bars Divine dark chocolate
150g unsalted butter, very soft
150g caster sugar
6 large free range eggs
150g plain flour
1/2 teaspoon baking powder
a pinch of salt

For the glaze
4 tablespoons apricot conserve
1 tablespoon water
1 teaspoon lemon juice

For the ganache
2 x 100g bars Divine dark chocolate
125ml double cream

23cm springclip tin, greased and base-lined

Heat the oven to 170C/325F/Gas 3.

For the sponge: break up the chocolate and put it into a heatproof bowl and melt gently (see page 16). Remove the bowl from the heat and leave to cool. Meanwhile, put the soft butter into the bowl of a food mixer and beat, using the whisk attachment, until very creamy. Add half of the sugar and beat again until very light and fluffy.

Separate the eggs, putting the whites into another mixing bowl, and beat the yolks into the creamed mixture one at a time, beating well after each addition. On low speed beat the cooled chocolate into the mixture. Sift the flour, baking powder and salt onto the mixture and gently fold in using a large metal spoon.

Whip the egg whites until stiff then beat in the rest of the sugar a tablespoon at a time to make a stiff glossy meringue. Add about a quarter of the meringue to the chocolate mixture and mix in well to soften the mixture and then carefully fold in the rest of the meringue in three batches. Spoon the mixture into the tin, spread evenly then make a slight hollow in the centre so the sponge rises evenly. Bake in the heated oven for 1 hour or until a skewer inserted into the centre comes out clean. Set the tin on a wire cooling rack and leave to cool for 10 minutes then carefully unclip the tin and remove the base and lining paper. Leave to cool completely.

Meanwhile, make the glaze: put the apricot conserve, water and lemon juice into a small pan and heat gently, stirring constantly. As soon as the mixture boils remove the pan from the heat and push the mixture through a sieve into a small bowl. Turn the cooled sponge cake upside down onto a wire rack – the flat surface will be easier to cover with ganache. Brush the hot glaze over the top and sides of the sponge (some chefs in Austria prefer to split the sponge in half horizontally then sandwich the two halves with more glaze). Leave to cool on the rack.

To make the ganache: break up the chocolate, reserving 8 squares for the decoration. Put the rest of the chocolate into a heatproof bowl. Heat the cream until steaming and then pour over the chocolate and stir gently until melted and smooth. Pour the ganache onto the cake and spread over the top and sides. Leave until set in a cool place (but not the fridge). Finally, to decorate with the letter S – melt the reserved chocolate, spoon into a greaseproof-paper icing bag and pipe the letter on top of the cake. Serve with whipped cream.

Store in an airtight container in a cool place and eat within a week.

STEVIE'S VERY NUTTY CAKE

My daughter Stevie is crazy about nuts and came up with this cake for her birthday; it combines all her favourite flavours – coffee and dark chocolate plus loads of Fairtrade nuts. With the help of an electric mixer, and a food processor for the chopping, the cake is easily put together and doesn't need a topping or filling.

MAKES 1 LARGE CAKE

200g blanched hazelnuts
1 x 100g bar Divine dark chocolate
200g walnut pieces
2 tablespoons Fairtrade instant coffee powder or granules
250g unsalted butter, very soft
250g caster sugar
4 large free range eggs
100g plain flour
1 teaspoon baking powder
icing sugar for dusting

23cm springclip or 20.5cm square tin, greased and base-lined

Heat the oven to 160C/325F/Gas 3.

Put the hazelnuts into an ovenproof dish and toast in the heated oven until golden, about 7–10 minutes. Leave to cool then put them into the bowl of a food processor. Break up the chocolate into squares and add to the bowl. Run the machine to make a fine powder. Add the walnuts pieces and 'pulse' the machine just for a second to roughly chop them – they should not be in very small pieces. Set aside until needed.

Dissolve the coffee in a tablespoon of boiling water, leave to cool until needed.

Put the soft butter and the sugar into the bowl of a food mixer. Beat thoroughly using the whisk attachment until pale and creamy. Beat in the eggs one at a time, beating well after each addition.

Stir in the chocolate mixture followed by the flour and baking powder, then finally the coffee liquid. When thoroughly combined transfer the mixture to the tin and spread evenly. Bake in the heated oven for 1 hour until firm to the touch. Run a round-bladed knife around the inside of the tin to loosen the cake but do not unclip the tin. Leave to cool completely on a wire rack then remove the tin.

Wrap and keep overnight before cutting. The cake deepens in flavour on keeping – it is at its best a couple of days after baking but will keep up to a week in an airtight container. Serve dusted with icing sugar.

WHITE CHOCOLATE STRAWBERRY CREAM CAKE

This lovely cake is made with white chocolate which helps make a surprisingly light sponge; it has a filling of strawberries flavoured with orange and white chocolate – the perfect cake for eating in the garden on a summer day.

MAKES 1 LARGE CAKE

For the sponge

1½ x 100g bars Divine white
   chocolate (150g)
200g unsalted butter, diced
3 large free range eggs, at room
   temperature
150g caster sugar
the grated zest ½ unwaxed
   orange
200g self-raising flour

For the filling

500g ripe strawberries (250g for
   filling and 250g for topping)
the grated zest and juice
   ½ unwaxed orange
1 tablespoon caster sugar
1 x 100g bar Divine white
   chocolate
150ml double or whipping cream,
   whipped
icing sugar for dusting

2 x 20.5cm sponge sandwich
   tins, greased and base-lined

Heat the oven to 180C/350F/Gas 4.

To make the sponge, break up the chocolate and melt very gently (see page 16) with the butter. Remove the bowl from the heat and leave to cool until needed.

Break the eggs into the bowl of a food mixer. Add the sugar and orange zest. Using the whisk attachment, whisk on full power for about 4 minutes or until the mixture is extremely thick and foamy. It's ready when the whisk leaves a ribbon-like trail of mixture when you lift it out of the mixture. Gently stir the chocolate mixture then whisk it briefly into the egg mixture. Turn off the power as soon as it is combined to avoid over-mixing. Add the flour and gently fold in using a large metal spoon. Divide the mixture between the two tins, and spread evenly.

Bake in the heated oven for 20 minutes until a light golden brown and the sponges spring back when gently pressed. Run a round-bladed knife around the inside of the tins, just to loosen the sponges, turn out onto a wire rack and leave to cool completely.

To make the filling, wipe the strawberries and save half of the good-looking ones for decoration. Thinly slice the rest into a bowl. Add the orange zest and juice, and the sugar and mix gently. Leave for 10 minutes for the flavours to develop. Grate the white chocolate and gently fold half into the whipped cream. Save the rest for the decoration.

To assemble, set one sponge on a serving plate and spoon on the strawberries and juice. Cover with the chocolate cream then top with the second sponge. Decorate with the reserved strawberries and grated chocolate and dust with icing sugar, serve.

The assembled cake can be stored in an airtight container in the fridge for 24 hours.

BALSAMIC AND CHOCOLATE CAKE

I found this egg and dairy-free recipe, which I have slightly adapted, on the back of a very good bottle of balsamic vinegar I was given. It may sound a slightly strange combination of flavours but it really is well worth trying. In summer it makes a great dessert if you add a bowl of mascarpone and really ripe figs cut into quarters.

MAKES 1 LARGE CAKE

100g Divine cocoa
350g plain flour
2 teaspoons baking powder
a good pinch of salt
350g caster sugar
250ml light olive oil
300ml warm water
2 tablespoons good quality
    balsamic vinegar
1 tablespoon white wine vinegar
mascarpone and ripe figs to
    serve

23cm springclip tin, greased and
    base-lined

Heat the oven to 180C/350F/Gas 4.

Sift the cocoa, flour, baking powder, salt and sugar into a mixing bowl.

Gently whisk the oil and water in a measuring jug, and pour onto the flour mixture. Stir well with a wooden spoon until thoroughly combined. Add the balsamic and wine vinegars and stir until well mixed. Spoon into the tin and spread evenly.

Bake in the heated oven for 40 minutes until firm to the touch but still soft in the centre, then turn off the oven but leave the cake inside for a further 10 minutes.

Remove the cake from the oven and set on a wire cooling rack and leave to cool for 30 minutes. Unclip the tin and serve, still slightly warm with the mascarpone and ripe figs.

The cake can also be left to cool then stored in an airtight container and is best eaten warm, within 2 days.

CHOCOLATE AMARETTI CAKE

This is another favourite cake from Italy. The strong almond flavour of the biscuits is the perfect match with the strong dark chocolate. It is both moist and rich, yet avoids being heavy or cloying – a combination of good quality chocolate and just enough liqueur (although you could use water if you prefer).

MAKES 1 MEDIUM CAKE

1 x 100g bar Divine dark chocolate
100g amaretti biscuits (the crisp rather than the soft kind)
100g plain flour
225g unsalted butter, softened
175g caster sugar
5 large free range eggs, separated
1 tablespoon Amaretto liqueur or lukewarm water
Divine cocoa powder for dusting

23cm springclip tin, greased and base-lined

Heat the oven to 180C/350F/Gas 4.

Break up the chocolate and put into the bowl of a food processor. Run the machine to make a fine powder. Add the amaretti biscuits and run the machine again until the mixture is fine. Add the flour then run the machine or 'pulse' briefly just to combine the ingredients. Set aside until needed.

Put the soft butter and sugar into the bowl of a food mixer and beat, with the whisk attachment, until light and creamy. Beat in the yolks, one at a time, beating after each addition. Stir in the chocolate mixture and the Amaretto or warm water.

In another bowl, whisk the egg whites until they form stiff peaks. Using a large metal spoon, fold the whites into the chocolate mixture in three batches. When thoroughly combined spoon the mixture into the prepared tin. Bake in the heated oven for about 40 minutes or until firm to the touch.

Remove the tin from the oven and run a round-bladed knife around the inside of the tin to loosen the cake. Carefully unclip the tin and leave the cake to cool on a wire rack. Dust with cocoa powder just before serving with whipped cream.

Store in an airtight container and eat within 4 days.

CHOCOLATE PASSION CAKE

It's impossible to resist a good passion cake with its light open texture and moreish flavour. I've added cocoa to the traditional recipe to make a truly yummy version even more difficult to resist. For the best result use good cream cheese, not the reduced-fat or 'bargain' variety.

MAKES 1 MEDIUM CAKE

For the sponge
3 large free range eggs
175g caster sugar
200ml sunflower oil
250g finely grated carrots (about 5 medium)
200g plain flour
3 tablespoons Divine cocoa powder
1 tablespoon baking powder
1 teaspoon ground cinnamon
1 teaspoon ground ginger
125g walnut pieces or chopped pecans

For the filling and topping
100g unsalted butter, very soft
100g good quality cream cheese
$\frac{1}{2}$ teaspoon vanilla essence
300g icing sugar, sifted
5 tablespoons Divine cocoa powder, sifted
2 tablespoons walnut pieces or chopped pecans to decorate

2 x 20.5cm sandwich tins, greased and base-lined

Heat the oven to 180C/350F/Gas 4.

Put the eggs and sugar into the bowl of a food mixer and beat, with the whisk attachment, until very light and frothy. Gradually beat in the oil. Using a large metal spoon, stir in the carrots. Sift the flour, cocoa, baking powder, cinnamon and ginger into the bowl and stir in. Once thoroughly combined mix in the nuts. Transfer the mixture to the prepared tins, dividing it evenly. Bake in the heated oven for 25 minutes or until firm to the touch. Turn out the sponges on to a wire rack and leave to cool completely.

Meanwhile, make the filling and topping: put the soft butter, cream cheese, vanilla, icing sugar and cocoa into the bowl of a food mixer and beat, on low speed, until very smooth and creamy. Use about half to sandwich the sponges, then spread the rest on top. Scatter over the nuts.

The cake will taste at its best if kept for a day before cutting. Store in an airtight container and eat within 5 days.

EASY MARBLED CAKE WITH WHITE CHOCOLATE ICING

The marbling effect always looks so attractive in this classic cake made from a creamed sponge, or pound cake mixture, but this recipe has the added twist of a creamy white chocolate topping that lifts it out of the ordinary.

MAKES 1 LARGE CAKE

For the cake
225g unsalted butter, very soft
225g caster sugar
1 teaspoon vanilla essence
225g self-raising flour
4 large free range eggs, at room
    temperature
3 tablespoons Divine cocoa
2 tablespoons milk, at room
    temperature

For the icing
100g bar Divine White chocolate
25g unsalted butter, very soft

1 loaf tin 900g, greased and
    base-lined

Heat the oven to 180C/350F/Gas 4.

Put the soft butter, sugar, vanilla, flour and eggs into the bowl of a food mixer. Whisk until the mixture is smooth, pale and creamy. Spoon half the mixture into another bowl. Sift the cocoa onto the remaining portion of cake mixture, add the milk and whisk again until just combined.

Put alternate spoonfuls of the two mixtures into the prepared tin, until both bowls are empty. Bang the tin on the work surface to knock out any air pockets, then use the handle of a teaspoon (or use a chopstick) to marble and swirl the two mixtures. Bake in the heated oven for 1 hour, or until a skewer inserted in the cake comes out clean. Remove the tin from the oven and leave to cool on a wire rack. Carefully remove the cake from the tin and set on a plate.

To make the icing: gently melt the bar of white chocolate. Remove the bowl from the heat and stir in the butter. Spread the icing over the cake and leave until firm. Serve thickly sliced.

Store in an airtight container and eat within 5 days. The un-iced cake can be frozen for up to a month.

DIVINE   HEAVENLY CHOCOLATE RECIPES

GATEAU MOCHA

The name Mocha comes from the Yemeni port of Moka, on the Red Sea, which became known for shipping the fine Arabian coffee produced in that area. Today it's known as either a hot drink made from a combination of coffee and chocolate or something flavoured with these ingredients. Here, three layers of chocolate and coffee sponge cake are layered with whipped chocolate-coffee cream then covered with a thick, shiny icing of chocolate ganache.

MAKES 1 LARGE CAKE

For the sponge
175g unsalted butter, softened
175g caster sugar
3 large free range eggs, at room temperature
150g self-raising flour
5 tablespoons Divine cocoa powder
½ teaspoon baking powder
1 tablespoon instant coffee (powder or granules not freshly made from beans) dissolved in 2 tablespoons warm water

For the filling
1 x 100g bar Divine coffee chocolate
125ml double cream

For the icing
1 x 100g bar Divine dark chocolate
100ml double cream

3 x 20.5cm sandwich tins, greased and base-lined

Heat the oven to 180C/350F/Gas 4.

Put the soft butter into the bowl of a food mixer. Beat with the whisk attachment until very creamy then add the sugar and beat well until fluffy and light. Gradually beat in the eggs, beating well after each addition. Sift the flour, cocoa, and baking powder into the bowl, add the coffee liquid and gently fold in using a large metal spoon. Divide the mixture equally between the three tins, spreading it evenly. Bake in the heated oven for 10–12 minutes until the mixture springs back when gently pressed. Turn out the cakes onto a wire rack and leave to cool completely.

To make the filling: break up the coffee chocolate and put into the bowl of a food mixer. Heat the cream until steaming hot but not quite boiling then pour over the chocolate and stir gently until melted and smooth. Leave to cool then chill thoroughly, about 30 minutes, but remove from the fridge before starting to set. Whip the cream until soft peaks form then use to sandwich the cakes.

To make the icing: break up the dark chocolate and put into a heatproof bowl. Heat the cream until steaming hot, then pour over the chocolate and stir gently until melted and smooth. Pour over the cake and gently spread over the top and down the sides, working the chocolate as little as possible to keep the glossy finish. Put into a cool place (but avoid the fridge unless the weather is very hot) until set.

Store in an airtight container in a cool place and eat within 3 days.

PANETTONE

I make this at Christmas ready for those late breakfasts and brunches, when all anyone wants is a large coffee and a slice of something special to celebrate the holiday. The very fine, delicate cake-like crumb and texture of this festive Italian yeast bread is the result of several risings, so allow plenty of time. A large food mixer does all the hard work.

MAKES 1 MEDIUM LOAF

350g strong white bread flour
1 x 7g sachet easy-blend dried yeast
3 large free range eggs, at room temperature
2 large free range yolks, at room temperature
75g caster sugar
1/2 teaspoon salt
grated zest of 1 unwaxed orange
grated zest of 1 unwaxed lemon
175g unsalted butter, very soft
75g sultanas
50g candied peel, very finely chopped
1/2 x 100g bar (50g) Divine orange milk chocolate, very finely chopped
40g unsalted butter, melted, for brushing
extra flour for working

15cm round deep cake tin (or coffee tin), greased and lined (base and sides, so paper extends 5cm above the height of the tin)

Put half of the flour into the bowl of a food mixer. Add the yeast and combine using the dough hook attachment. Beat the 3 whole eggs until just mixed then add to the yeast mixture. On low speed work the ingredients together to make a very thick, smooth batter. Cover the bowl with a lid or cling film and leave in a warm spot until doubled in size – about 1 hour.

Mix the two egg yolks into the batter then add the rest of the flour, the sugar, salt, plus the orange and lemon zest. Mix the ingredients together on low speed to form a very soft and sticky dough. Cut up the butter into small pieces and gradually work into the dough, still at low speed. Knead the dough in the machine on low speed for 3–4 minutes until it is no longer streaky but looks smooth and silky.

Cover the bowl as before and leave in a warm but not hot spot until doubled in size – about 2 hours. Flour your knuckles then punch down the dough to deflate it. Cover again and leave to rise as before until doubled in size – about an hour this time. Turn out the dough onto a lightly floured work surface and punch down.

Combine the sultanas with the chopped peel and chocolate in a small bowl. Add a teaspoon of flour and toss gently – this helps prevent them sticking together in clumps in the dough. Scatter the mixture over the dough and gently knead in with your hands. Shape the dough into a ball and gently drop into the prepared tin. Cut a cross in the top of the dough with the tip of a sharp knife. Cover the top of the tin loosely then leave in a warm spot until doubled in size – about 1 hour. Meanwhile, heat the oven to 200C/400F/Gas 6.

Brush the top of the loaf with plenty of melted butter then bake in the heated oven for 10 minutes. Brush again with melted butter, then reduce the oven temperature to 180C/350F/Gas 4 and bake for about 40 minutes, or until a skewer inserted into the centre comes out clean. Set the tin on a wire cooling rack and leave to cool for 15 minutes (the crust of the loaf will be very fragile) then gently turn out and leave to cool completely before slicing.

Store in an airtight container and eat within 5 days, or toast.

WINDFALL PEAR CAKE

A wonderful autumn cake recipe that is perfect for using up windfalls or odd-sized pears from the farmers' market. The orange milk chocolate works really well with the pears, and it is lovely warm from the oven for tea, or with whipped cream for a satisfyingly cosy dessert.

MAKES 1 MEDIUM CAKE

500g pears, fairly firm (about 4)
175g self-raising flour
225g caster sugar
225g unsalted butter, at room temperature
1 unwaxed orange, washed
½ a 100g bar Divine Orange milk chocolate
2 large free range eggs
Demerara sugar for sprinkling

23cm springclip tin, greased and base-lined

Heat the oven to 190C/375F/Gas 5.

Peel the pears, quarter and remove the cores, then cut into dice. Set aside until needed. Mix the flour with the sugar in a mixing bowl. Cut the butter into small pieces and toss with the flour. Using the tips of your fingers briefly rub the butter into the flour so there are still some visible flakes of butter, rather than fine breadcrumbs.

Add the pears and mix gently. Grate the zest of the orange into the bowl. Roughly chop the orange chocolate and add. Again, gently stir the mixture just to combine the ingredients. Squeeze the juice from the orange, add 4 tablespoons to the eggs and beat until mixed. Stir into the other ingredients to make a fairly stiff cake mixture.

Transfer to the prepared tin and spread evenly. Sprinkle with a little Demerara sugar then set the tin on the baking tray and bake in the heated oven for about 1 hour or until a skewer inserted into the centre of the cake comes out clean. Remove the tin from the oven and run a round-bladed knife all around the inside of the tin just to loosen the cake. Carefully unclip the tin and leave the cake to cool on a wire rack.

Serve at room temperature, with whipped cream or clotted cream, or warm with a hot chocolate sauce (see page 133).

Store in an airtight container and eat within 4 days.

RASPBERRY CHOCOLATE GATEAU

A big, glamorous layer-cake for when you want to pull out all the stops! Rich and velvety smooth raspberry buttercream, sandwiched between flourless chocolate sponge encased in dark chocolate ganache icing, and then decorated with plenty of fresh raspberries. Heavenly.

MAKES 1 LARGE CAKE

For the sponge
9 large free range eggs, at room temperature, separated
200g caster sugar
90g Divine cocoa powder

For the filling
225g fresh or frozen raspberries
50g caster sugar
1 tablespoon crème de framboise or raspberry liqueur, optional
175g unsalted butter, at room temperature
175g icing sugar
2 large free range egg yolks

For the ganache
200g Divine dark chocolate
200ml double cream
a few fresh raspberries to decorate

3 x 20.5cm sponge tins, greased and base-lined

Heat the oven to 180C/350F/Gas 4.

First make the sponge: put the egg yolks into the bowl of a food mixer. Add the sugar and whisk for 3–4 minutes until very thick and pale, and a thick ribbon-like trail of mixture falls back into the bowl when the whisk is lifted.

Sift the cocoa into the bowl and gently fold in – it will be quite difficult to work in, so after several strokes leave it and, in a separate very clean bowl, whisk the egg whites until stiff. Add a small portion of the whites to the yolk mixture and stir in – this time it will mix quite easily. Fold in the remaining whites in three batches to make a thick mousse-like batter. Divide the mixture evenly between the three tins then bake in the heated oven for about 20 minutes until just firm to the touch. Remove the tins from the oven and leave to cool completely on a wire rack before turning out.

Meanwhile, make the filling: put the raspberries and sugar into a pan and simmer gently, stirring frequently until very thick – about 10 minutes. Push the mixture through a sieve to remove the seeds then leave to cool. Beat the butter until creamy using a food mixer. Sift the icing sugar into the bowl, add the egg yolks and beat until thick and smooth. Add the cooled raspberry purée and raspberry liqueur and beat thoroughly for a couple of minutes until very light and fluffy. Use the filling to sandwich the three sponges, then set the cake on a plate and chill briefly while making the icing.

Break up the dark chocolate and put into a heatproof bowl. Heat the cream until steaming hot then pour over the chocolate. Leave for a minute then stir gently until smooth and melted. Spoon the ganache onto the cake and spread it evenly over the top and down the sides. Leave to set in a cool spot then decorate with the raspberries.

Best eaten within 2 days. Store in an airtight container in a cool place.

TRY THIS TOO...   GATEAU ARABICA

Make up the sponge cakes as above. Make the filling without the raspberry purée but adding 3 tablespoons of cold espresso coffee, plus a little coffee liqueur to taste. Cover the cake with the ganache then decorate with chocolate coffee beans.

STEM GINGER AND CHOCOLATE CHUNK CAKE

I adore the combination of warm, spicy glacé ginger and really good quality milk chocolate, and this is one of the easiest ginger cake recipes you could imagine – everything is made in a single saucepan.

MAKES 1 MEDIUM CAKE

50g light muscovado sugar
2 tablespoons black treacle
75g honey
85g unsalted butter, diced
100ml milk
75g chopped glacé ginger
1 large free range egg, beaten
225g plain flour
1/4 teaspoon sea salt
1 teaspoon bicarbonate of soda
1 x 100g bar Divine milk
    chocolate

450g loaf tin (tin size about 18 x
    12 x 7cm high), greased and
    base-lined

Heat the oven to 180C/350F/Gas 4.

Put the sugar, black treacle, honey, butter, milk and the chopped ginger into a saucepan large enough to easily hold all the ingredients. Set over a low heat and melt gently.

Remove the pan from the heat, leave to cool for a couple of minutes and then stir in the egg. Sift the flour, salt and bicarbonate of soda into the pan and mix in well. Break up the chocolate, breaking each square in half, stir in. Spoon the mixture into the tin and spread evenly.

Bake in the heated oven for 45–50 minutes until a skewer inserted into the centre comes out clean. Set the tin on a wire cooling rack and leave to cool completely before turning out.

Serve thickly sliced. Best eaten within 3 days. Store in an airtight container.

RICH CHOCOLATE NUT BREAD

Like chocolate brioche but without the same amount of effort or time! A large mixer will do all the kneading for you, and the dough only needs one rising – in the tin. Try eating lightly toasted with butter or cream cheese, or it can be used in bread and butter pudding.

MAKES 1 LARGE LOAF

2 x 100g bars Divine dark chocolate
300ml milk, hot but not boiling
100g blanched hazelnuts, lightly toasted and halved
500g unbleached white bread flour
1 teaspoon salt
150g unsalted butter, at room temperature, diced
50g light muscovado sugar
7g sachet easy-blend dried yeast

900g loaf tin, well greased and gently warmed

Break up the chocolate into squares. Put half into a heatproof bowl and pour over the hot milk and leave to melt stirring frequently. Mix the rest of the chocolate with the nuts and set aside until needed.

Put the flour and salt into the bowl of a food mixer or a large mixing bowl. Add the diced butter and rub into the flour using the tips of your fingers until the mixture looks like fine crumbs. Mix in the sugar and yeast and make a well in the centre. Add the just-warm milk then mix well using the dough hook attachment of the mixer (on the lowest speed) or your hands, to make very soft and slightly sticky dough. Then knead the dough thoroughly either in the mixer, still on low speed, for 4 minutes or turn out onto the work surface and knead and stretch the dough for 5 minutes. Sprinkle the chocolate and nut mixture over the dough and work in. When thoroughly combined lift the dough into the tin and press down to eliminate any air bubbles and make a neat loaf shape. Place the tin in a large plastic bag, inflate slightly and tie closed. Leave in a warm place until doubled in size – 1–1$\frac{1}{2}$ hours.

Meanwhile heat the oven to 180C/350F/Gas 4. Uncover the loaf and bake in the heated oven for 45 minutes – to test if the loaf is cooked, turn out onto a wire rack and tap the underside with your knuckles. If it sounds hollow the loaf is cooked, if there is a dull 'thud' then return the loaf to the oven (without the tin) for 5 minutes and test again. Leave on a wire rack to cool completely.

Best eaten within 2 days or slightly longer if using for bread and butter pudding.

DIVINE   HEAVENLY CHOCOLATE RECIPES

THE BIG QUICK CAKE

When you need to make a really impressive cake in a hurry this is the recipe! It is the perfect chocolate cake for any occasion – you can add any decoration you choose, candles, sprinkles, chocolate coffee beans, or my favourite, Divine Chocolate Coins. Just make sure the butter is really soft (but not about to melt) and remove the eggs from the fridge a good hour before starting.

MAKES 1 LARGE CAKE

For the cake
75g Divine cocoa
200g self-raising flour
1 teaspoon baking powder
a good pinch of salt
250g light muscovado sugar
250g unsalted butter, very soft
6 medium free range eggs, at
   room temperature

For the icing
1 x 100g bar Divine coffee milk
   chocolate
100g unsalted butter, diced, at
   room temperature
100g icing sugar
1 tablespoon Divine cocoa

23cm springclip tin, greased and
   base-lined

Heat the oven to 180C/350F/Gas 4.

Sift the cocoa, flour, baking powder, salt and sugar into the bowl of a food mixer.

Add the soft butter and the eggs. Using the whisk attachment, beat at medium speed all the ingredients together until smooth and light, scraping down the bowl from time to time.

Spoon the mixture into the prepared tin and spread evenly. Bake in the heated oven for about 50 minutes, until firm to the touch and a skewer inserted into the centre of the cake comes out clean. Carefully unclip the tin and leave the cake to cool on a wire rack.

To make the icing: break up the chocolate and melt very gently (see page 16). Remove the bowl from the heat and stir in the butter. Sift the icing sugar and cocoa into the bowl and mix in to make a smooth icing. Stir until the icing is thick enough to spread over the top and sides of the cake. Once the cake is iced decorate as you choose. Leave lightly covered in a cool place until firm. The cake is at its best the next day when it will cut easily.

DESSERTS

BAKLAVA

The classic baklava doesn't include chocolate, and I didn't think I could ever improve on the recipe, but I just adore this version where dark chocolate is added to the lightly cooked nuts before layering with the fine sheets of filo pastry. As with many recipes that combine chocolate and spices, the flavour develops over time. Use a good quality filo pastry and follow the package instructions carefully for thawing and storing – the thin sheets become as dry as parchment if not kept covered.

CUTS INTO 30

400g filo pastry

For the filling
100g blanched almonds
100g walnut pieces
100g shelled unsalted pistachios
3 tablespoons caster sugar
1 x 100g bar Divine dark chocolate
175g unsalted butter, melted

For the syrup
330g caster sugar
300ml water
2 cinnamon sticks
1 tablespoon lemon juice
3 tablespoons Greek honey

22 x 30cm roasting tin or baking tin

If the pastry is frozen, defrost according to the packet instructions. Once unwrapped, keep the pastry covered with cling film or a damp tea towel to prevent it from drying out.

To make the filling, put all the nuts into a food processor and chop until they resemble coarse breadcrumbs. Tip into a heavy-based dry frying pan and stir over low heat until the nuts are just starting to colour – about 4–5 minutes. Take care as they will quickly scorch so it's best to slightly undercook them. Remove the pan from the heat, stir in the sugar and leave to cool completely. Using a sharp knife or processor chop the dark chocolate into small pieces the same size as the nuts. Stir into the cooled nuts. Heat the oven to 180C/350F/Gas 4.

Lightly brush the inside of the tin with melted butter then begin the layering process. Cover the base of the tin with a layer of filo (you may need one or two sheets slightly overlapping depending on your brand of pastry). Brush lightly with butter, then continue layering with filo and brushing with butter until you have six layers of pastry in the tin. Spread a third of the chocolate nut mixture over the pastry. Cover with two more layers of buttered filo. Spread half the remaining chocolate mixture on top then cover with two more layers of buttered filo and then finally spread the rest of the chocolate mixture evenly over the pastry in the tin. Fold in any overhanging edges of pastry then butter the rest of the pastry sheets and set on top. If necessary trim any overhanging pastry with kitchen scissors.

Using a sharp knife, cut the baklava into pieces (squares or diamonds) as it is easier to do this now rather then when the pastry is baked. Sprinkle the top lightly with cold water then bake in the heated oven for 15 minutes. Increase the heat to 190C/375F/Gas 5 and bake for a further 15 minutes until crisp and golden.

While the baklava is baking, make the syrup – put the sugar and water into a saucepan and heat gently until the sugar has dissolved. Bring to the boil then add the cinnamon sticks, lemon juice and honey. Simmer gently for 10 minutes then remove from the heat and leave to stand for 10 minutes.

DIVINE HEAVENLY CHOCOLATE RECIPES

Remove the baklava from the oven and pour over the hot syrup. Lave to cool and to absorb the syrup. Remove the cinnamon sticks before serving. Best kept overnight before serving.

Store in an airtight container and eat within 5 days.

BLACK FOREST ROULADE

All the elements of the classic gâteau – dark but richly flavoured and light flourless sponge, morello cherries, kirsch, whipped cream, chocolate and more kirsch – but in a roulade. A wonderful combination and easy to prepare and serve.

SERVES 6–8

For the sponge
6 large free range eggs, at room temperature, separated
140g icing sugar, sifted
50g Divine cocoa powder

For the filling and topping
1 x 465g jar morello cherries in kirsch syrup (290g drained) or morello cherries in fruit syrup plus 3 tablespoons kirsch
1 x 100g bar Divine dark chocolate
125ml double cream
200ml whipping cream, well-chilled
icing sugar for dusting

Swiss roll tin, baking tin or oven tray about 25 x 32 cm, greased and lined with non-stick baking parchment

Heat the oven to 190C/375F/Gas 5.

To make the sponge: put the egg yolks and 100g of the sifted icing sugar into the bowl of a food mixer and beat until light and mousse-like – the whisk should leave a ribbon-like trail when lifted out of the bowl. Sift the cocoa into the bowl and gently fold in with a large metal spoon. Put the egg whites into another bowl and whisk until soft peaks form. Whisk in the remaining sugar one tablespoon at a time to make a stiff meringue. Fold into the yolk mixture in three batches. Pour the mixture into the prepared tin and gently spread evenly.

Bake in the heated oven for 10–12 minutes until just firm to the touch. Meanwhile, cover a wire cooling rack with a damp tea towel topped with a sheet of non-stick baking parchment dusted with caster sugar. Tip the cooked sponge onto the rack, lift off the tray and peel off the lining paper and leave to cool completely.

Meanwhile, make the whipped cream filling and the dark chocolate and cream topping: put a bowl in the fridge or freezer to chill ready for whipping the cream. Drain the cherries thoroughly, reserving the kirsch syrup. Set both aside until needed (note: if using 'plain' fruit syrup plus kirsch, mix the kirsch with 4 tablespoons of fruit syrup). Break up the dark chocolate, and put into a heatproof bowl. Heat the double cream until steaming hot but not boiling then pour over the chocolate. Stir gently until melted and smooth. Leave to cool then stir in 4 tablespoons of the kirsch syrup. Beat well with a wooden spoon and chill until thick enough to spread – 15–30 minutes.

Whip the chilled whipping cream in the chilled bowl until soft peaks form. Add 2 tablespoons of the reserved kirsch syrup and whip briefly until almost stiff. Sprinkle 1 tablespoon of the reserved kirsch syrup over the sponge then spread with the cream, leaving a 2cm border all around. Top with the drained cherries (save a few for decoration) then roll up from one narrow end using the paper to help you lift and guide the roll into shape.

Set the roll on a serving plate. Spread the chocolate topping over the roulade, leaving the ends free, then use a round-bladed knife to run lines down the length to resemble the bark of a log. Gently set the reserved cherries on top and chill for 30 minutes or until ready to serve. The flavour improves if kept overnight. If not serving immediately put into a sealed container or cover tightly.

Can be kept in the fridge for up to 3 days. Dust with icing sugar before serving.

CHOCOLATE BANOFFI PIE

Better the original Banoffi Pie – a pastry case filled with a fudgy toffee mixture then topped with bananas and whipped cream flavoured with coffee, invented in 1972 by Ian Dowding and Nigel Mackenzie at the Hungry Monk restaurant in Sussex (it is still on the menu) – but do try this combination of chocolate shortcrust pastry, toffee cream, bananas, then a thick topping of whipped milk chocolate cream. I think it rivals the original.

SERVES 8–10

For the pastry
150g plain flour
2 tablespoons Divine cocoa
   powder
4 tablespoons icing sugar
100g unsalted butter, chilled and
   diced
1 large free range egg yolk
2–3 tablespoons cold water ·

For the chocolate cream
1 x 100g bar Divine milk
   chocolate
300ml double cream

For the toffee cream
150ml double cream
50g unsalted butter, diced
100g caster sugar
3 tablespoons water
2 medium bananas
cocoa powder for dusting

24cm loose-based flan tin

To make the pastry: put the flour, cocoa, and icing sugar into the bowl of a food processor. Run the machine briefly just to combine. Add the diced butter and process until the mixture looks sandy. Add the egg yolk and a couple of tablespoons of cold water and process to make a ball of dough. If the mixture is dry and crumbly add a little extra water. Wrap and chill the dough for 30 minutes.

Turn out onto a lightly floured work surface and roll out to a circle about 30cm across. Use to line the flan tin, then prick the base and chill for 30 minutes to prevent the pastry shrinking. Meanwhile, heat the oven to 180C/350F/Gas 4. Bake the pastry blind (line the inside of the pastry case with a sheet of non-stick baking paper, fill with baking beans) for 10 minutes then remove the paper and beans and bake for a further 8–10 minutes until firm. Remove from the oven and leave to cool.

Make the chocolate cream: break up the chocolate and put into the bowl of a food mixer. Heat the cream until steaming hot, but not boiling, then pour over the chocolate and stir gently until completely melted and smooth. Leave to cool and then chill thoroughly – at least 4 hours.

Make the toffee cream: heat the cream until steaming hot but not boiling, then stir in the diced butter. Keep warm while making the caramel. Gently heat the sugar and water in a small heavy pan, stirring frequently until melted. Then bring to the boil and boil steadily without stirring, but shaking and swirling the pan frequently, until the syrup turns a rich chestnut brown. Remove the pan from the heat, cover your hand with an oven glove and pour in the warm cream – the mixture will splutter so take care. Stir gently to melt any lumps of caramel then leave to cool. Beat well with a wooden spoon then chill for 30 minutes until thick. Spoon into the pastry case and spread evenly. Peel and thinly slice the bananas and arrange on top. Whip the cream using the whisk attachment of the food mixer until soft peaks form then spread over the bananas. Chill for about 2 hours then dust with cocoa before serving.

DIVINE HEAVENLY CHOCOLATE RECIPES

GALETTE DES ROIS AU CHOCOLAT

This is the traditional Twelfth Night cake from France, eaten warm on January 6th to celebrate Epiphany, the festival of the arrival of the three kings to Jesus' birthplace with their gifts. A dried or ceramic bean is hidden in the filling, and who ever gets it in their portion becomes king or queen for the day. Obviously if you do decide to keep with tradition and include the ceramic bean do take care!

SERVES 8—10

700g puff pastry (made with pure butter)

For the filling
1 x 100g bar Divine dark chocolate
100g unsalted butter, softened
100g caster sugar
1 whole large free range egg
1 large free range egg yolk
100g ground almonds
1 dried or ceramic bean

To glaze
1 free range egg beaten with a pinch of salt
a gold paper or cardboard crown

baking tray, greased

If necessary defrost the pastry according to the packet instructions. Keep the pastry, well-covered, in the fridge until needed.

Break up the chocolate, put into a heatproof bowl and melt gently (see page 16). Remove the bowl from the heat and leave to cool. Put the softened butter into the bowl of a mixer and beat with the whisk attachment until very creamy. Add the sugar and beat until thoroughly combined. Beat in the whole egg, followed by the yolk and beat until the mixture is very light. Stir in the ground almonds followed by the cooled chocolate. Cover and chill for 15 minutes.

Roll out the pastry fairly thinly – about 0.3cm – then cut out two circles each 25cm across using a plate or pan lid as a guide. Set one circle onto the baking tray. Spoon the filling onto the pastry, mounding it slightly in the centre, and leaving a 2.5cm border of pastry all around the edge. Push the bean into the filling, not too close to the centre (to avoid confusion).

Brush the pastry border with beaten egg glaze then gently lie the second circle on top. Press the edges together firmly to seal and then 'scallop' them by pressing the tips of two fingers down on to the edge, then with the back of a knife pull the pastry back between your fingers. Repeat all around the edge. Brush the top of the pastry very lightly with egg glaze. Chill for 20 minutes. Meanwhile, heat the oven to 220C/425F/Gas 7. Brush again with the glaze then score the top in a diamond pattern with the tip of a sharp knife, without cutting through the pastry. Make a couple of small holes in the centre to allow steam to escape. Bake in the heated oven for 25 minutes until golden, puffed and crisp.

Serve warm rather than piping hot from the oven, with the gold crown on top. If you're making the cake in advance reheat gently before serving.

MARBLED CHOCOLATE CREAM MERINGUES

The usual meringue of egg whites and sugar is marbled here with melted chocolate and filled with whipped cream for a good treat. A piece of non-stick baking parchment or a flexible silicon sheet is necessary to stop the mixture sticking to the baking tray.

MAKES 8 PAIRS

For the meringue
1 x 100g bar Divine dark
   chocolate
3 large free range egg whites
a pinch of cream of tartar
175g caster sugar
Divine cocoa powder for dusting

For the filling
200ml double cream, well-chilled
½ teaspoon vanilla essence

2 baking trays lined with non-stick
   baking paper

Heat the oven to 120C/250F/Gas ½

Break up the dark chocolate and put into a heatproof bowl. Melt gently (see page 16) then remove the bowl form the heat and leave to cool, stirring occasionally, until needed. Put the egg whites into the bowl of a food mixer. Whisk until almost stiff then tip in the sugar and whisk briefly to make a very stiff glossy meringue.

Drizzle the chocolate over the meringue, and using a large metal spoon, gently fold the chocolate into the meringue using just 2 or 3 strokes to give a streaky marbled affect. With a large dessert spoon shape the meringues into 16 mounds on the prepared trays. Dust with cocoa powder and then bake in the heated oven for 2 hours until firm. Leave to cool and then gently peel off the lining paper.

Meanwhile, chill a bowl for whipping the cream. To make the filling: put the chilled cream into the chilled bowl. Add the vanilla and then whip until thick and firm. Use to sandwich the meringues. Set on a serving plate. Cover lightly and chill until ready to serve. Dust with cocoa powder at the last minute.

The meringues can be kept in an airtight container in the fridge for up to 3 days.

OLD-FASHIONED HOT CHOCOLATE PUDDING WITH CHOCOLATE CUSTARD

Baked rather than steamed, and with a real homemade chocolate custard this is what my grandmother made on Fridays, to eat after the inevitable fish dish. It may not be as glamorous as some recipes in this book but it is still a family favourite.

SERVES 4–6

For the pudding
125g unsalted butter, very soft
125g castor sugar
3 large free range eggs, at room
   temperature
100g self-raising flour
½ teaspoon baking powder
3 tablespoons Divine cocoa
   powder
½ teaspoon vanilla essence
30g ground almonds
1 tablespoon milk

For the custard
450ml creamy milk
3 tablespoons Divine cocoa
   powder
4 tablespoons caster sugar
1 tablespoon cornflour
2 large free range egg yolks

18cm soufflé dish or deep baking
   dish, greased, and a roasting
   tin

Heat the oven to 160C/325F/Gas 3.

Half fill the roasting tin with water and set in the oven to heat up. Put the soft butter, caster sugar, eggs, flour, baking powder, cocoa powder, vanilla, almonds and milk into the bowl of a food mixer and beat well until very smooth and thoroughly combined (you can also do this using a mixing bowl and wooden spoon). Spoon the mixture into the prepared soufflé dish.

Cut a large square of foil and butter one side. Fold the foil down the middle to make a pleat (so the pudding can rise), then cover the dish buttered-side down, making sure the foil is tightly fitting. Put the dish into the water-filled roasting tin and bake for 1 hour until firm to the touch.

Meanwhile, make the custard: heat all but 2 tablespoons of the milk in a medium-sized non-stick pan. Sift the cocoa, sugar and cornflour into a heatproof bowl. Add the yolks and reserved milk then stir to make a thick, smooth paste. Stir in the hot milk then pour the mixture back into the pan and stir gently over a low heat until the custard thickens – don't let the mixture boil or the eggs will scramble. Pour into a jug and serve hot with the pudding.

HAZELNUT CHOCOLATE SPONGE PUDDING

I like sponge puddings, especially chocolate ones, but I find steaming the traditional way a bit of a fiddle. Baked sponges taste just as good. This one is served with a creamy chocolate sauce rather than custard.

CUTS INTO 8–10 PIECES

For the sponge
4 tablespoons Divine cocoa
100ml boiling water
200g unsalted butter, very soft
200g light muscovado sugar
3 large free range eggs
200g self-raising flour
1 x 100g bar Divine milk chocolate with chopped hazelnuts
50g hazelnuts, roughly chopped

For the sauce
125ml single cream
1 x 100g bar Divine dark chocolate
25g unsalted butter

20.5 x 25.5cm brownie tin or cake tin, greased and base-lined

Heat the oven to 180C/350F/Gas 4.

Mix the cocoa with the boiling water in a heatproof bowl and stir until smooth. Leave to cool until needed. Put the soft butter, sugar, eggs and flour into the bowl of a food mixer and beat until smooth and thoroughly mixed. Add the cocoa mixture and beat again until combined. Break the bar of hazelnut chocolate into squares and stir into the sponge mixture. Spoon into the prepared tin and spread evenly. Scatter the chopped nuts over the top then bake in the heated oven for 20 minutes or until just firm to the touch.

While the sponge is baking, make the chocolate sauce: heat the cream in a small pan until steaming. Remove the pan from the heat. Break up the bar of plain chocolate and add the squares to the cream. Stir gently until smooth then stir in the butter. Keep warm.

Cut the hot sponge into squares and set on individual plates, pour over a little warm sauce and serve immediately, with the rest of the sauce in a jug. Any left over sponge and sauce can be eaten gently reheated, or at room temperature as a cake.

DIVINE HEAVENLY CHOCOLATE RECIPES

ROAST PEACHES WITH WHITE CHOCOLATE SAUCE

An elegant dish perfect for a summer meal – enjoy with a glass of chilled prosecco.

SERVES 4–6

For the peaches
4 to 6 ripe peaches
40g unsalted butter, melted
3 tablespoons caster sugar

For the sauce
1 x100g bar Divine white
*   chocolate*
175ml milk
1 vanilla pod
3 large free range egg yolks
20g caster sugar

oven proof dish large enough to
*   hold the peaches upright,*
*   greased*

Heat the oven to 200C/400F/Gas 6.

With a small sharp knife make a small nick in the skin of each peach right at the top. Put the peaches in a large heatproof bowl and pour over enough boiling water to cover, leave for 10 seconds. Remove the peaches one at a time and peel off the skins – if they are ripe the water will have loosened them so they slip off easily, unripe peaches will need longer in the water. Roll the peaches one at a time in the melted butter then in the sugar and stand them upright, slightly apart, in the prepared dish. Roast in the heated oven for 25 minutes until golden and soft but not falling apart. Remove and leave to cool slightly.

Meanwhile, make the sauce: break up the white chocolate and melt gently (see page 16). Remove the bowl from the heat and leave to cool until needed. Put the milk into a medium-sized pan. Split the vanilla pod lengthways and add to the pan. Gently heat the milk until it steams and then remove the pan from the heat.

Put the egg yolks and sugar into a heatproof bowl and beat well with a wooden spoon until very pale – about a minute. Pour on the hot milk, stirring constantly. Remove the vanilla pod and scrape some of the black seeds into the egg mixture. Pour the egg mixture back into the pan and cook gently over a low heat, stirring constantly with the wooden spoon until the mixture thickens slightly – the mixture must not come to the boil or it will turn to scrambled eggs. Remove the pan from the heat and stir in the melted chocolate.

Serve the peaches slightly warm with the warm sauce.

LA TORTA DI CIOCCOLATA

Piedmonte, in the far northwest of Italy is one place to go for chocolate and nuts. Turin is famous for its gianduitto, a chocolate made from dark chocolate and toasted hazelnuts, other towns combine chocolate with almonds or walnuts or a combination. This is my version of the classic Italian chocolate and nut dessert. A rich unbaked confection it is very easy and wonderful to have ready in the fridge at Christmas time. Serve small slices after dinner with coffee, or cut into larger wedges and eat with ice-cream or whipped cream with brandy as a dessert.

MAKES 1 LARGE TORTA – SERVES ABOUT 12

100g blanched hazelnuts
100g blanched almonds
200g plain crisp butter biscuits – such as Petit Beurre
2 x 100g bars Divine dark chocolate
2 large free range eggs, at room temperature
2 large free range egg yolks, at room temperature
6 tablespoons caster sugar
150g unsalted butter
Divine cocoa powder, for dusting

23cm springclip tin, lightly oiled and base-lined

Heat the oven to 180C/350F/Gas 4.

Tip the hazelnuts and almonds into an ovenproof dish and toast them in the heated oven for 5–7 minutes until lightly browned. Remove the dish from the oven and leave to cool. Chop the nuts very coarsely – you can do this in a processor but here it's much better to use a large knife. Put the biscuits into a food processor and reduce to coarse crumbs (you can also do this by putting the biscuits into a plastic bag and smashing them with a rolling pin).

Break up the chocolate, put it into a heatproof bowl and melt gently (see page 16). Remove the bowl from the heat and leave to cool until needed. Put the whole eggs and the egg yolks into the bowl of a food mixer. Whisk until combined then add the sugar and whisk vigorously for about 5 minutes until the mixture is really pale, thick and mousse-like, and when the whisk is lifted out of the mixture a thick ribbon-like trail of mixture falls back into the bowl.

Heat the butter in a small pan until hot and bubbling. Pour the very hot butter onto the egg mixture in a thin stream while still whisking at full speed. Whisk in the melted chocolate. Remove the bowl from the mixer and fold in the chopped nuts and biscuit crumbs with a large metal spoon. Turn the mixture in to the prepared tin and spread evenly. Cover the top of the tin with plastic film then chill for at least 3 hours, preferably overnight before serving.

When ready to serve, unclip the tin and set the torta on a serving plate. Dust with cocoa and serve chilled. Store, well covered, in the fridge and eat within 3 days.

TARTE AU CHOCOLAT

The crisp pastry in this delicious tarte is a foil for the velvety smooth and deeply rich filling of eggs, cream and dark chocolate. All it needs is a jug of thick cream to serve.

SERVES 8–10

For the pastry
175g plain flour
a pinch of salt
2 tablespoons icing sugar
125g unsalted butter, chilled and
    diced
1 large free range egg yolk
1 tablespoon cold water

For the filling and topping
300ml double cream
2 x 100g bars Divine dark
    chocolate
2 large free range eggs, at room
    temperature

To finish
White or dark chocolate shavings

24cm loose-based flan tin and a
    baking tray

To make the pastry: put the flour, salt, icing sugar and diced butter into the bowl of a food processor. Run the machine until the mixture looks like fine crumbs. Add the yolk and water and 'pulse' the machine until the dough comes together in a ball. Remove from the bowl, wrap and chill for 30 minutes. Roll out the dough on a lightly floured work surface to a circle about 4mm thick and 30cm across. Wrap the pastry around the rolling pin and lift it into the flan tin. Gently press the pastry onto the base and sides of the tin. Trim off the excess pastry then prick the base well with a fork and chill for 30 minutes.

Meanwhile, heat the oven to 180C/350F/Gas 4. Line the pastry case with a piece of crumbled up greaseproof paper and fill with either dried beans, ceramic baking beans, or coins, then bake in the heated oven for 10 minutes. Carefully remove the paper and beans and cook the pastry case for another 5 minutes until the base is barely coloured. Remove from the oven and set on a baking tray.

To make the filling: bring the cream to the boil in a medium saucepan. Remove the pan from the heat. Break up the two bars of dark chocolate and stir into the hot cream. Stir gently until melted and very smooth. Break the eggs into a mixing bowl and whisk very briefly until slightly frothy then whisk in the chocolate cream. When thoroughly combined pour into the pastry case. Bake in the heated oven for 20 minutes until the filling is barely firm – it will carry on cooking for a few minutes after you remove from the oven. Remove from the oven and leave to cool on a wire rack.

When ready to serve remove the tarte from the pastry case and set on a serving plate. Decorate with the chocolate shavings. Keep tightly covered in the fridge for up to 4 days. Remove from the fridge about an hour before serving to 'come to'.

DIVINE DOUBLE CHOCOLATE TORTE

I was sent this recipe from Washington D.C. by Marion Ocquaye Pitcher. A native of Ghana, Marion attended culinary school in England. She is the Head Pastry Chef at Washington's renowned 'Old Ebbit Grill' where she made this Torte for the launch of Divine's US sister company, Divine Chocolate Inc. She is a great enthusiast for Divine chocolate. She says it's better to use for her dessert creations because of its great flavour and perfect texture. Her recipe uses few ingredients and is simple to make, just melt and mix then pour the mixture into a loaf tin and bake. Once cooled and chilled overnight the torte is then covered with a milk chocolate glaze. The result is very smooth and dense with a secret flavouring – Bourbon whiskey.

SERVES ABOUT 10

For the torte
2 x 100g bars plus $1/4$ bar 25g
   (225g) Divine dark chocolate
225g unsalted butter, diced
150g caster sugar
2 tablespoons Bourbon
4 large free range eggs, at room
   temperature
$1/2$ teaspoon vanilla essence

For the milk chocolate glaze
1 x100g bar plus $1/2$ bar (150g)
   Divine milk chocolate
5 tablespoons double cream
1 teaspoon Bourbon

450g loaf tin, oiled and
   completely lined with non-stick
   baking paper, plus a roasting tin

Heat the oven to 180C/350F/Gas 4

Fill the roasting tin up to two thirds full of water and put it into the oven to heat up – it will act as a water bath (or bain-marie) for cooking the torte. Break up the dark chocolate and put it into a large heatproof bowl. Add the diced butter, sugar and Bourbon. Set the bowl over a pan of steaming hot, but not boiling water, and leave to melt gently, stirring occasionally.

Remove the bowl from the heat and leave to cool for 2 minutes. Whisk the eggs and vanilla until just mixed then whisk into the chocolate mixture. When the mixture is very smooth pour it into the prepared tin. Place the tin in the water bath in the oven and bake until just firm – 50–60 minutes. Remove the tin from the water bath and leave to cool completely then cover tightly and chill in the fridge overnight.

Next day make the milk chocolate glaze. Break up the milk chocolate and put into a heatproof bowl. Heat the cream until boiling then pour over the chocolate. Leave for 3–5 minutes then stir gently until the chocolate has melted and the mixture is smooth. Stir in the Bourbon. Leave for about 15 minutes until the mixture has thickened but is still pourable.

Turn out the torte onto a serving plate and remove the lining paper. Spoon the milk chocolate glaze over the torte and spread it evenly over the top and sides. Return the torte to the fridge until the glaze is firm – about an hour. Serve cut into very thin slices with fresh berries and whipped cream.

Best eaten within 5 days.

WARM CHOCOLATE TORTE

This flourless torte has a light moist texture and plenty of flavour. Perfect served with fresh berries and cream.

SERVES 6–8

125g blanched hazelnuts
3 x 45g bars Divine dark
 chocolate
125g unsalted butter, very soft
100g caster sugar
4 large free range eggs,
 separated
icing sugar for dusting
whipped cream and berries for
 serving

23cm springclip tin, greased and
 base-lined

Heat the oven to 200C/400F/Gas 6.

Tip the hazelnuts into an ovenproof dish and toast in the heated oven for about 5 minutes until a very pale gold colour – take care to watch them, if they become too brown they will become bitter. Remove from the oven, leave to cool for 5 minutes then tip into a food processor and grind to make a fine powder. Set aside until needed. Break up the chocolate and melt gently (see page 16), then remove the bowl from the heat and leave to cool until needed.

Put the soft butter and sugar into the bowl of a food mixer fitted with the whisk attachment, and beat until very pale and creamy. Beat in the egg yolks, one at a time, beating well after each addition. Beat in the cooled melted chocolate, then, on slow speed, the ground hazelnuts.

Put the egg whites into another, spotlessly clean and grease-free bowl, and whisk until soft peaks form. Using a large metal spoon gently fold the egg whites into the chocolate mixture in three batches. Spoon the mixture into the prepared tin and spread evenly. Bake in the heated oven for 10 minutes then reduce the heat to 180C/350F/Gas 4 and bake for a further 5–7 minutes until just firm to the touch – the centre should be slightly soft. Remove the tin from the oven and set on a wire cooling rack. Run a knife around the inside of the tin but do not unclip. Leave the tart to cool for 15 minutes then gently remove it from the tin.

Serve warm, dusted with icing sugar along with a bowl of whipped cream plus fresh berries.

DIVINE HEAVENLY CHOCOLATE RECIPES

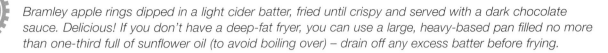

APPLE CIDER FRITTERS WITH CHOCOLATE SAUCE

Bramley apple rings dipped in a light cider batter, fried until crispy and served with a dark chocolate sauce. Delicious! If you don't have a deep-fat fryer, you can use a large, heavy-based pan filled no more than one-third full of sunflower oil (to avoid boiling over) – drain off any excess batter before frying.

SERVES 4–6

For the sauce
1 x 100g bar Divine dark
  chocolate
50g unsalted butter, diced
100ml water

3 medium to large Bramley
  cooking apples
3 tablespoons caster sugar
1 teaspoon ground cinnamon

For the batter
100g plain flour
1 large free range egg yolk
2 large free range egg whites
150ml cider
sunflower oil for deep-frying
icing sugar for dusting

To make the sauce: break up the chocolate, put it into a small heavy pan with the butter and water and heat gently and stir frequently until melted. Whisk gently to give a glossy and smooth sauce. Keep warm until needed.

Peel the apples, remove the core then cut into thick 1cm rings. Mix together the sugar and cinnamon and toss the apple rings in the sugar. Put the flour into a mixing bowl, and add the egg yolk. Put the whites into another bowl. Add the cider to flour mixture and whisk to make a smooth thick batter.

Heat the oil in a deep fryer to 190C/375F or a heavy-based pan (see above). Whip the egg whites until stiff then gently fold into the batter. Dip the rings into the batter and immediately fry in batches, maybe two at a time, cooking them for 3–4 minutes turning them frequently. Once crisp and golden remove from the oil and drain on kitchen paper. Dust with icing sugar. Serve immediately with the warm sauce.

BOURBON STREET BEIGNETS

New Orleans is famed not just for its music but for its food too – and it's hard to miss these heavenly beignets (or little pillows) of fried dough. The fancy restaurants serve savoury and seafood versions but the street cafés are the best place to have sweet ones heavily dusted with icing sugar, along with a cup of coffee. Beignets can be made from yeast dough, like doughnuts, or a sweet light and fluffy nut batter as in this recipe which I serve with a spicy chocolate sauce and sticky fried bananas.

SERVES 4–6

For the beignets
50g pecan pieces
150g plain flour
2 tablespoons caster sugar
1½ teaspoons baking powder
½ teaspoon ground cinnamon
a pinch of salt
2 large free range eggs
100ml water
oil for deep-frying

For the chocolate sauce
1 x 100g bar Divine dark chocolate
175ml single cream
1 teaspoon – 1 tablespoon Bourbon (to taste)
1 teaspoon instant coffee powder or granules
1cm cube fresh root ginger, peeled and finely grated
1 teaspoon icing sugar
a pinch cayenne pepper

For the banana sauce
2 medium bananas
25g unsalted butter
2 tablespoons light muscovado sugar
1 teaspoon ground cinnamon
1 teaspoon – 1 tablespoon Bourbon (to taste)
icing sugar for dusting

First make the batter for the beignets. Heat the oven to 180C/350F/Gas4.

Put the pecans into an ovenproof dish and toast in the heated oven for 10–12 minutes until starting to colour. Remove, leave to cool then put into the bowl of a food processor and grind to a fine powder. Sift the flour, sugar, baking powder, cinnamon and salt into a mixing bowl. Stir in the ground nuts then add the eggs and water and beat all the ingredients together to make a thick, smooth batter. Cover the bowl and chill for at least 30 minutes (but no more than 3 hours).

Meanwhile, make the sauces. Break up the chocolate and put it into a small heavy pan with the cream, Bourbon, coffee, ginger, sugar and cayenne. Set over a low heat and heat gently, stirring constantly until melted and smooth. Taste and adjust the flavourings as needed. Keep warm until ready to serve.

For the banana sauce: first peel and thinly slice the bananas. Heat the butter in a non-stick frying pan or sauté pan. Add the bananas, sugar, cinnamon and Bourbon and heat gently, stirring frequently for a couple of minutes until sticky. Keep warm until ready to serve.

To cook the beignets: heat the oil in a deep-fat fryer to 170C/325F. Using a tablespoon of batter for each beignet, fry in small batches, gently dropping the batter into the hot oil and cooking for about 3–4 minutes, turning them frequently, until a good golden brown. Drain on kitchen paper, dust with icing sugar and serve immediately with the two warm sauces.

BLACK AND WHITE CHOCOLATE ROULADE

This rich, light textured flourless sponge is made from melted chocolate and is filled with a white chocolate mousse, you can add rum or brandy as you wish. As is true with so many chocolate recipes the assembled roulade is even better eaten the next day. For perfect presentation, slice with a large sharp knife wiped and dipped in hot water between slices.

SERVES 6–8

For the cake
2 x 100g bars Divine dark chocolate
6 medium free range eggs
200g caster sugar
1 teaspoon vanilla essence or 2 tablespoons rum or brandy

For the filling
1 x 100g bar Divine white chocolate
200ml double cream
1 teaspoon vanilla essence or 1 tablespoon rum or brandy

To finish
Icing sugar for dusting
Plain or white chocolate for curls or shavings
Fresh berries or chestnuts in syrup or brandy (drained)

20.5 x 30 cm Swiss roll tin, greased and base-lined

Heat the oven to 180C/350F/Gas 4.

Break up the chocolate and melt gently (see page 16). Remove the bowl from the heat and leave to cool until needed. Crack the eggs, putting the yolks into the bowl of a food mixer, and the whites into another bowl. Add the sugar and the vanilla (or rum or brandy) to the yolks and beat using the whisk attachment until very thick and pale – about 3 minutes. Stir in the chocolate. Whisk the egg whites until they form soft peaks. Add a spoonful to the chocolate mixture and mix in thoroughly to soften the mixture. Add the remaining whites in three batches, gently folding them in with a large metal spoon. Pour the mixture into the prepared tin and spread evenly.

Bake in the heated oven for 15 minutes until just firm to the touch. Leave to cool for 2 minutes. Put a sheet of non-stick baking parchment onto a wire cooling rack and sprinkle with a little caster sugar. Tip the cake out of the tin onto the paper. Peel off the paper that has been lining the tin then gently roll up the cake, from one long side, using the parchment to help lift the cake into shape. Leave the cake to cool completely, wrapped in the parchment.

To make the filling: break up the white chocolate and melt gently (see page 16). Remove the bowl from the heat and leave to cool for a couple of minutes.

Whip the cream with the vanilla (or rum or brandy) until soft peaks form. Gently fold in the melted chocolate. Unwrap the cake – don't worry if it has cracks or even large splits, this is quite normal. Spread with the cream then gently re-roll. Wrap in parchment paper to help retain the shape and then chill for at least an hour or overnight.

To serve, remove the paper and transfer to a serving plate then dust the roulade with icing sugar. Add chocolate shavings and fresh berries or chestnuts and serve.

DIVINE HEAVENLY CHOCOLATE RECIPES

CHOCOLATE BRIOCHE PUDDING

The ultimate in comfort food – similar to bread and butter pudding but richer, and made with chocolate – bliss!

SERVES 4–6

350m single cream
350ml milk
1 vanilla bean, split lengthways
1 x 100g bar Divine dark chocolate
1 whole free range egg
5 large free range egg yolks
50g caster sugar
100g – about 7 slices – brioche or challah
50g unsalted butter, very soft

1 baking dish about 1.5l, plus a roasting tin to act as a water bath

Put the cream, milk and vanilla bean into a medium pan. Heat slowly, stirring frequently, until the mixture just comes to the boil. Remove the pan from the heat and leave for 20 minutes for the vanilla to infuse.

Meanwhile, break up the chocolate and set aside until needed. Put the yolks and sugar into a heatproof bowl and mix well. Spread the bread with the soft butter and cut each slice in half diagonally. Arrange the slices, slightly overlapping, in the baking dish, buttered side uppermost. Reheat the milk mixture until steaming hot. Remove from the heat, discard the vanilla bean then add the chocolate pieces and stir until smooth and melted. Pour this mixture onto the egg yolks and stir or whisk until thoroughly combined. Pour the chocolate egg custard over the bread, gently pressing down the bread so it is thoroughly covered. Leave for 15 minutes for the bread to absorb the liquid.

Meanwhile, heat the oven to 160C/325F/Gas 3 and half fill the roasting tin with water and put it into the oven to heat up. Set the pudding into the water bath in the oven and bake for 35–40 minutes until firm. Remove the dish from the water, and leave for about 30 minutes before serving.

CHOCOLATE STUFFED FRENCH TOAST

A lovely homely dish, using thick slices of soft brioche or challah bread with a hidden centre of chocolate, then dipped in a slightly spicy creamy egg mix and quickly fried.

SERVES 4

1 x 100g bar Divine dark or milk
  chocolate or orange milk
  chocolate
4 thick (about 3cm) slices of
  challah or brioche
4 large free range eggs
3 tablespoons double or thick
  single cream
1 tablespoon caster sugar
$\frac{1}{4}$ teaspoon grated nutmeg
$\frac{1}{4}$ teaspoon ground cinnamon
about 50g unsalted butter, for
  frying

To finish
3 tablespoons caster sugar
1 teaspoon ground cinnamon

Break up the chocolate – you will need about 16 squares. Cut each slice of bread in half (to make 8 pieces) then make a small horizontal slit or pocket in each piece, using a small sharp knife. Carefully insert about 2 squares into each piece – if the slices are very large you may be able to fit a bit more into each pocket.

Beat the eggs with the cream, sugar, nutmeg, and cinnamon in a shallow bowl.

Heat the butter in a non-stick frying pan. Once foaming, dip the pieces of bread into the egg mixture one at a time, to thoroughly coat, then put into the hot butter. You may need to fry the bread in two batches. Cook until golden on both sides – about 2 minutes on each side. While the bread is frying, combine the sugar and cinnamon. Remove the bread from the pan, arrange on a serving plate, sprinkle with the cinnamon sugar and serve immediately.

DIVINE   HEAVENLY CHOCOLATE RECIPES

HAZELNUT, BERRIES AND CREAM SHORTCAKE

A pretty and easy dessert for when you need something impressive in a hurry. A very simple chocolate and hazelnut shortbread (made in a food processor), acts as a perfect base for the creamy topping which in turn is offset by the tart, colourful fresh berries.

SERVES 6

For the shortcake
2 tablespoons Divine cocoa
100g plain flour
a good pinch of salt
50g caster sugar
50g hazelnuts, lightly roasted
100g unsalted butter, chilled and
    diced
1 large free range egg yolk

For the sauce
250g raspberries
2 tablespoons caster sugar, or to
    taste
1 tablespoon lemon juice

For the topping
200ml crème fraîche (full or half-
    fat) or extra thick double cream
250g mixed berries – raspberries,
    blackberries, strawberries,
    tayberries, blueberries
icing sugar for dusting

1 baking tray, greased

Heat the oven to 180C/350F/Gas 4.

Put the cocoa, flour, salt, sugar and hazelnuts into the bowl of a food processor. Run the machine until the mixture looks like coarse sand. Add the pieces of butter and run the machine again for a few seconds until the mixture looks like coarse crumbs. Add the yolk and run the machine until the mixture comes together to make a ball of dough.

Tip the dough out onto the prepared baking tray. Dip your fingers in flour then press out the dough to make a flat disc about 20cm across. Prick the dough with a fork then press the back of the fork onto the rim of the disc to decorate. Bake in the heated oven for 20 minutes until just firm and golden brown around the edge. Carefully transfer to a wire cooling rack and leave until cold.

Meanwhile, make the sauce: put the raspberries, sugar and lemon juice in the bowl of a food processor and run the machine to make a thick purée. Taste and add more sugar or lemon juice if desired. Chill until needed.

When ready to serve, put the shortcake onto a serving plate. Spread the cream on top then decorate with the berries. Spoon a little of the sauce over the top and dust with icing sugar. Serve immediately with the rest of the sauce in a jug.

FLOURLESS RICH FRENCH TORTE

This is even richer than the Warm Chocolate Torte (page 118). It is made with ground almonds rather than flour, for a light moist crumb, but the overwhelming flavour is dark chocolate. It doesn't need any icing or sauce but is wonderful served slightly warm with a strong coffee ice-cream.

SERVES 8–10

2 x 100g bars Divine dark
 chocolate
200g unsalted butter, diced
4 large free range eggs, at room
 temperature, separated
100g caster sugar
50g light muscovado sugar
100g ground almonds
icing sugar for dusting

23cm springclip tin, greased and
 base-lined

Heat the oven to 180C/350F/Gas 4.

Break up the chocolate, put into a heatproof bowl with the diced butter and melt gently (see page 16). Remove the bowl from the heat and leave to cool until needed.

Put the egg yolks and both sugars into the bowl of a food mixer. Beat with the whisk attachment until very thick and fluffy. Gently stir in the cooled chocolate mixture and the ground almonds.

Whip the egg whites until stiff. Using a large metal spoon, very gently fold the whites into the chocolate mixture in three batches. Spoon into the prepared tin and spread evenly. Bake in the heated oven for 30 minutes until the centre is barely set. Remove the tin from the oven and set on a wire rack. Leave to cool for 15 minutes and then carefully remove the torte from the tin. Dust with icing sugar and serve just warm or at room temperature. Best eaten within 2 days.

LEMON AND CHOCOLATE TART

I adore lemon tart, and when I discovered a French patisserie that made a selection of fruit tarts with a layer of chocolate I couldn't resist trying the combination. It works!

MAKES 1 TART — SERVES 8

For the sweet pastry
175g plain flour
a good pinch of salt
3 tablespoons icing sugar
125g unsalted butter, chilled and diced
1 large egg yolk
1½ to 2 tablespoons cold water
1 x 45g bar Divine dark chocolate

For the filling
The grated zest of 2 unwaxed lemons
125ml lemon juice (from about 3 lemons)
225g caster sugar
4 large free range eggs, lightly beaten
150g unsalted butter, diced

To decorate
Divine cocoa for dusting or grated Divine dark chocolate or a little extra melted Divine dark chocolate

24cm loose-based flan tin

Make the pastry in the food processor: put the flour, salt, icing sugar and diced butter into the bowl of the processor. Run the machine until the mixture looks like fine crumbs. Add the yolk and one and half tablespoons of water and 'pulse' the machine until the dough comes together in a ball. If there are dry crumbs or the dough seems stiff and dry add a little extra water. Remove the dough from the bowl, wrap and chill for 30 minutes.

Roll out the dough on a lightly floured work-surface to a circle about 4mm thick and 30cm across. Wrap the pastry around the rolling pin and lift it into the flan tin. Gently press the pastry onto the base and sides of the tin. Trim off the excess pastry, then prick the base well with a fork and chill for 30 minutes. Meanwhile, heat the oven to 180C/350F/Gas 4. Line the pastry case with a piece of crumpled up greaseproof paper and fill with dried beans, ceramic beans or coins then bake in the heated oven for 10 minutes. Carefully remove the paper and beans and cook the pastry case for another 5 minutes until firm and barely coloured. Remove from the oven and leave to cool. Break up the chocolate, put it into a heatproof bowl and melt gently (see page 16). Brush the chocolate inside the pastry case to evenly cover the base and sides. Leave to set while making the filling.

Put the lemon zest and juice, sugar, beaten eggs, and diced butter into a heatproof mixing bowl. Set over a pan of steaming water and stir gently until melted and smooth. Continue stirring for about 10 minutes or until the mixture thickens and looks like lemon curd. Remove the bowl from the heat and pour the mixture into a clean bowl (to prevent overcooking and scrambling the filling). Leave to cool completely, and then spoon the filling into the pastry case. Chill thoroughly – at least 4 hours – then decorate by dusting with cocoa powder, sprinkling with grated chocolate or shavings, or with piped swirls or spirals of melted chocolate (using a greaseproof paper icing bag, or plastic bag with the corner snipped off).

If not serving immediately cover tightly and keep in the fridge. Eat within 3 days.

DIVINE HEAVENLY CHOCOLATE RECIPES

TIRAMISU

The classic Italian dessert of coffee, brandy and chocolate but with a twist. Instead of the traditional plain sponge fingers, layered between the mascarpone 'mousse' I've used homemade chocolate ones.

SERVES 8

For the sponge fingers
1 x 100g bar Divine dark
   chocolate
1 tablespoon instant coffee
   (powder or granules) dissolved
   in 1 tablespoon warm water
3 large free range eggs,
   separated
5 tablespoons caster sugar

For the mascarpone mixture
125ml espresso or strong coffee
4 tablespoons brandy
3 large free range eggs,
   separated
5 tablespoons caster sugar
250g mascarpone
1 x 100g bar Divine dark
   chocolate or Divine coffee milk
   chocolate

Swiss roll tin about 20.5 x
   30.5cm greased and base-lined
Large shallow serving dish or
   glass bowl

Heat the oven to 180C/350F/Gas 4.

For the sponge fingers: break up the chocolate, put into a large heatproof bowl with the coffee and melt very gently (see page 16). Remove the bowl from the heat and gently stir in the egg yolks. Whisk the egg whites until stiff then whisk in the sugar a tablespoon at a time. Gently fold the whites into the chocolate mixture in three batches. Don't over mix – it's better to have a few streaks than a flattened batter.

Pour the mixture into the tin and spread evenly. Bake in the heated oven for 10–13 minutes until just firm to the touch and the mixture has started to shrink away from the sides of the tin. Cover a wire cooling rack with a sheet of greaseproof paper and sprinkle with caster sugar, turn out the sponge onto the paper. Lift off the tin and the lining paper and leave to cool.

Cut the sponge in half lengthways, then across into fingers about 2.5cm wide. Arrange half the fingers in the base of the serving dish (I use a lasagne dish). Mix the coffee with the brandy. Spoon about half the coffee mix over the sponge fingers and leave to soak while you make the topping. Put the egg yolks into the bowl of a food mixer. Add 4 tablespoons of the sugar and whisk until very thick and light – about 3–4 minutes. Gently fold in the mascarpone. In another bowl stiffly whisk 2 egg whites. Add the last tablespoon of sugar and whisk in briefly. Fold the egg whites into the mascarpone mixture.

Finely chop the chocolate in a food processor. Spoon half the mascarpone mixture over the soaked sponge fingers. Scatter over half the chopped chocolate. Arrange the rest of the sponge fingers on top. Carefully spoon or brush the rest of the coffee mixture over the sponge fingers. Cover with the remaining mascarpone mixture, spreading it evenly, and then finish by scattering over the rest of the chopped chocolate. Cover the dish and chill until ready to serve – at least 2 hours.

Best eaten within 24 hours.

DESSERTS

HOT CHOCOLATE BRANDY SOUFFLE

This recipe was given to me by Anne Willan. Anne is the founder/owner of La Varenne, the legendary cooking school, originally in Paris, now based in her château in Burgundy. She had an award-winning French food series in the Observer Magazine in the '80s which is how I got to know her as I was the recipe tester. She has written many books on French food. This is like a hot chocolate mousse, very indulgent.

SERVES 4

3 x 45g bars Divine dark
  chocolate
150ml double cream
3 large free range eggs,
  separated plus 2 egg whites
2 tablespoons brandy
$\frac{1}{2}$ teaspoon vanilla essence
3 tablespoons caster sugar
icing sugar for sprinkling

1.25ml soufflé dish or 4 x 300ml
  soufflé dishes or oven-proof
  large coffee cups, a baking tray.

Brush the inside of the soufflé dish or dishes with melted butter, and sprinkle with caster sugar. Set on a baking tray. Break up the chocolate and put into a heavy-based pan with the cream. Set over a low heat and stir with a wooden spoon, until melted. Take the pan off the heat and beat the three egg yolks into the hot mixture so they cook and thicken it. Stir in the brandy and vanilla. The soufflé can be covered and kept at a cool room temperature for up to an hour at this point. Half an hour before serving, heat the oven to 220C/425F/Gas 7.

Put the five egg whites into the bowl of the food mixer and whip until stiff. Add the caster sugar and beat 20 seconds longer or until the mixture looks glossy. Gently heat the chocolate mixture until just hot to the touch then remove the pan from the heat. Stir in about a quarter of the whites just to loosen the mixture then add this mixture to the whites and carefully fold them together.

Spoon into the prepared dish (or dishes) and bake at once in the heated oven allowing 12–15 minutes for the large soufflé or 7–9 minutes for the smaller ones – the mixture should still be wobbly in the centre. Sprinkle with icing sugar and serve immediately.

TRY THIS TOO...

HOT CHOCOLATE COFFEE SOUFFLE

Replace the cream with 125ml strong black coffee, and omit the vanilla. The brandy can be replaced with Tia Maria.

PROFITEROLES

I just had to include this classic recipe for these versatile little choux pastry buns but I've included three different fillings to choose from – a simple whipped cream, a rich chocolate and coffee French pastry cream or a dark chocolate ice-cream. Then just before serving simply pour over either the dark chocolate or white chocolate warm sauce.

MAKES 32 – SERVES 8

For the choux pastry
185ml water
a pinch of salt
75g unsalted butter
100g plain flour
3 large free range eggs

For the crème Chantilly filling
200ml double cream, well chilled
1 tablespoon caster sugar
½ teaspoon vanilla essence

For mocha pastry cream filling
3 large free range egg yolks
50g caster sugar
2 tablespoons plain flour
1½ tablespoons cornflour
1 tablespoon instant coffee
1 tablespoon Divine cocoa powder
275ml creamy milk
125ml double or whipping cream
1 tablespoon icing sugar

For the ice-cream filling
500ml dark chocolate or white chocolate ice-cream (see page 33)

For the dark chocolate sauce
1 x 100g bar Divine dark chocolate
25g unsalted butter
2 tablespoons icing sugar
100ml water

For the white chocolate sauce
1 x 100g bar Divine white chocolate
100ml single cream

several baking trays, greased and dampened

To make the choux pastry buns: put the water, salt and butter in a medium-sized pan. Heat gently until the butter melts. Bring to the boil then immediately remove the pan from the heat and tip in all the flour. Beat vigorously with a wooden spoon – don't worry that the mixture will look like a complete mess at this point, it will soon come together to make a smooth heavy ball of dough. Return the pan to a low heat and beat for about 30 seconds to dry out the dough slightly. Turn the dough into the bowl of a food mixer and leave to cool until tepid. Meanwhile, heat the oven to 190C/375F/Gas 5. Beat the eggs just to combine then using the whisk attachment gradually beat into the dough, beating well after each addition and saving the last tablespoon of egg for glazing.

Put small balls of dough slightly apart on the prepared trays; you can either use a teaspoon or a pastry bag fitted with a 1.5cm plain tube, aiming to make them about 2.5cm across and 1.5cm high. Lightly brush the tops with the egg glaze then bake in the heated oven for 15–20 minutes until crisp and golden. Remove the trays from the oven and make a small hole in one side of each bun with a cocktail stick or skewer to let out the steam. Return the trays to the oven and bake for another 3–5 minutes until really crisp then transfer the buns to a wire rack and leave to cool completely.

To make the crème Chantilly filling: place the bowl of a food mixer and the whisk in the fridge to chill (if you have room) – this will help give you a stiffer cream which is less likely to split. Whisk the cream

(Continued on page 134)

DESSERTS

(Continued from page 133)

until soft peaks form. Add the sugar and vanilla and whisk briefly until just stiff. Use immediately or cover and chill for up to an hour.

To make the mocha pastry cream filling: beat the egg yolks with the sugar, flour, cornflour, coffee and cocoa in a heatproof bowl. Heat the milk in a medium-sized pan then pour onto the yolk mixture and stir well to combine. Tip the mixture back into the pan and cook stirring or whisking constantly until the mixture boils then beat or whisk vigorously until the mixture is thick and smooth. Turn into a bowl, press a damp piece of greaseproof paper on to the surface to prevent a skin forming and leave to cool completely. Whip the cream until soft peaks form. Add the sugar and whisk again until just stiff then stir into the cold pastry cream. Use immediately or cover and chill until needed – up to 12 hours.

If you are using the ice-cream filling: remove the ice-cream from the freezer and leave to soften just enough to form small balls using a teaspoon or melon-ball cutter. Set the 32 balls (one for each profiterole) on a baking tray lined with greaseproof or wax paper and return to the freezer until ready to serve.

To make the dark chocolate sauce: break up the chocolate and put it into a small heavy pan with the butter, icing sugar and water. Heat gently until melted then beat well with a whisk until smooth. Keep warm until ready to serve.

To make the white chocolate sauce: break up the chocolate and put it into a heatproof bowl. Melt very gently (see page 16) then remove the bowl from the heat. Heat the cream until steaming hot but not boiling then whisk onto the chocolate in a thin steady stream to make a smooth sauce. Keep warm until ready to serve.

To assemble the profiteroles: slit the choux buns open horizontally and fill with a spoonful of filling. Pile the buns in a dish and pour over a little sauce and serve immediately with the rest of the warm sauce in a jug.

STICKY UPSIDE-DOWN CHOCOLATE PEAR GINGERBREAD

Chocolate, pears and ginger make a wonderfully warming combination and this is one of those puddings to have at a weekend lunch when the weather turns chilly.

SERVES 6

For the topping
50g unsalted butter
100g light muscovado sugar
4 medium pears
50g walnut halves

For the gingerbread
100g self-raising flour
2 tablespoons Divine cocoa
$\frac{1}{2}$ teaspoon bicarbonate of soda
$\frac{1}{2}$ teaspoon ground cinnamon
$1\frac{1}{2}$ teaspoons ground ginger
$\frac{1}{2}$ teaspoon ground mixed spice
50g unsalted butter
50g light muscovado sugar
50g black treacle
50g golden syrup
100ml milk
1 large free range egg

20cm square cake tin, greased

Heat the oven to 180C/350F/Gas 4.

First make the topping: put the butter and sugar into a small pan and heat gently, stirring, until the butter has melted. Pour the mixture into the tin to make an even layer. Peel the pears, then halve them and scoop out the cores with a teaspoon, arrange in the tin, cut-side down. Scatter the walnuts in between. Set aside until needed.

To make the gingerbread – sift the flour, cocoa, bicarbonate of soda, cinnamon, ginger, and mixed spice into a mixing bowl. Put the butter, sugar, treacle and syrup into a small pan and heat gently, stirring, until the butter has melted. Pour into the flour mixture. Whisk the milk with the egg and add to the bowl. Mix well with a wooden spoon. Carefully spoon the gingerbread mixture over the pears and spread gently to cover evenly.

Bake in the heated oven for about 35 minutes until firm to the touch. Run a knife around the inside of the tin, then immediately turn out onto a large serving plate and serve warm with crème fraîche, custard or ice-cream. The turned out gingerbread can also be left to cool then covered tightly. Eat warm within 2 days.

CHEESECAKES

CREAMY CAPPUCCINO CHEESECAKE

A really creamy and deeply flavoured cheesecake. The base is a dark chocolate mocha biscuit-crumb combination which contrasts with the coffee filling. Look out for Fairtrade instant coffee to flavour the filling and choose top quality full-fat cream cheese.

MAKES 1 LARGE CHEESECAKE – SERVES 8–12

For the base
1 x 100g bar Divine coffee chocolate
50g unsalted butter, diced
200g digestive biscuits

For the filling
500g best quality cream cheese
125g light muscovado sugar
50g caster sugar
2 rounded teaspoons instant coffee dissolved in 1 tablespoon hot water
1 tablespoon Kahlua (optional)
2 large free range eggs

To finish
Divine cocoa powder for dusting

23cm spring-clip tin, greased, set a baking tray

Heat the oven to 160C/325F/Gas 3.

To make the base: break up the chocolate and melt very gently with the butter in a large heatproof mixing bowl (see page 16). Remove the bowl from the heat and stir gently until smooth. Put the biscuits into a plastic bag and crush with a rolling pin to make fine crumbs. Tip the crumbs into the melted chocolate, mix well and then tip the mixture into the prepared tin. Using the back of a spoon, press the mixture into the base of the tin and halfway up its sides. Chill until needed.

To make the filling: put the cream cheese, both sugars, dissolved coffee, Kahlua (if using) and the eggs into the bowl of a food processor and run the machine until the mixture is very smooth. Pour the filling into the tin set on the baking tray. Bake in the heated oven for 40 minutes until just set, then turn off the heat and leave the cheesecake to cool in the oven. When completely cold cover and chill overnight.

To serve, carefully unclip the tin and set the cheesecake on a serving plate. Dust heavily with cocoa.

Store, tightly covered, in the fridge and eat within 4 days.

DIVINE   HEAVENLY CHOCOLATE RECIPES

WHITE CHOCOLATE CHEESECAKE

This is a classic to rival even Lindy's world-famous cheesecakes in New York, in my opinion. A dark chocolate crumb base topped with a rich and creamy white chocolate filling. The orange and lemon zests, along with the slight saltiness of the cream cheese give a real tang to avoid any cloying.

MAKES 1 LARGE CHEESECAKE – SERVES 8–12

For the base
2 tablespoons Divine cocoa
75g unsalted butter, melted
150g digestives, crushed
50g caster sugar

For the filling
2 x 100g bars Divine white
    chocolate
3 tablespoons warm water
600g good quality cream cheese
75g caster sugar
grated zest of $\frac{1}{2}$ unwaxed orange
grated zest and juice of $\frac{1}{2}$
    unwaxed lemon
$\frac{1}{2}$ teaspoon vanilla essence
2 large free range eggs

To finish
Divine plain chocolate shavings or
    cocoa

23cm springclip tin, greased and
    base-lined, set on a baking tray

Heat the oven to 150C/300F/Gas 2.

Make the base first: mix the cocoa with the melted butter then stir in the biscuit crumbs and the sugar. When thoroughly combined tip the mixture into the tin and, using the back of a spoon, press firmly onto the base and about 2cm up the sides. Chill until needed.

Break up the white chocolate and melt gently with the water (see page 16). Remove the bowl from the heat, stir gently and leave to cool until needed. Put the cream cheese, sugar, orange zest, lemon juice and zest, vanilla and eggs into the bowl of a food processor. Run the machine until the mixture is very smooth, scraping down the sides from time to time. Add the melted chocolate and run the machine until thoroughly combined. Pour the mixture into the chilled base, then set the tin (on the baking tray) into the heated oven and bake for 40 minutes. Once cooked turn off the oven but do not remove the cheesecake and leave to cool for an hour. Then remove the tin, leave to cool completely then cover and chill overnight. When ready to serve, run a round-bladed knife inside the tin to loosen the cheesecake then unclip the tin. Decorate with plain chocolate shavings or dust with cocoa.

Store in an airtight container in the fridge and eat within 4 days.

MARBLED ITALIAN CHEESECAKE

If you love the combination of chocolate and the Italian amaretti, those small almondy round biscuits, then this is for you. Instead of using American-style cream cheese that some cheesecakes have, this one includes mascarpone, the soft Italian cheese with a creamy consistency that adds a lovely silky texture and great flavour.

MAKES 1 LARGE CHEESECAKE — SERVES 8–12

For the base
50g unsalted butter, melted
100g amaretti biscuits, crushed

For the white cream cheese mixture
250g mascarpone
100g caster sugar
1 tablespoon Amaretto liqueur
   or 1 teaspoon vanilla essence
1 large free range egg

For the dark chocolate mixture
3 x 100g bars Divine plain
   chocolate
150g unsalted butter, at room
   temperature, diced
3 large free range eggs
100g caster sugar
1 tablespoon Amaretto liqueur
   or 1 teaspoon vanilla essence

23cm springclip tin, greased and
   base-lined

Heat the oven to 150C/300F/Gas 2.

Make the base first: mix the melted butter with the biscuit crumbs, then tip the mixture into the tin and press onto the base using the back of a spoon, to make an even layer. Chill until needed.

To make the white cream cheese mixture: put the cream cheese into another mixer bowl or the bowl of a food processor. Add the sugar and liqueur or vanilla and beat or process until smooth. Add the egg and beat or process to make a smooth, thick batter (it will not be as thick as the dark mixture).

To make the dark chocolate mixture: break up the chocolate and melt gently (see page 16). Remove the bowl from the heat and stir in the pieces of butter, once smooth set aside until needed. Put the eggs, sugar and liqueur or vanilla into the bowl of an electric food mixer and whisk for 3–4 minutes until very thick, pale and fluffy. Whisk in the chocolate mixture. Set aside until needed.

To assemble: spoon half the dark mixture onto the base of the tin and spread evenly. Pour the white mixture on top and then drop spoonfuls of the remaining dark mixture into the tin. Gently marble and swirl the two mixes with the handle of a teaspoon.

Bake in the heated oven for 40 minutes until just firm to the touch. Leave the tin in the oven but turn it off and leave until cool. Remove the tin from the oven, cover and chill for 2 hours or overnight before removing the cheesecake from the tin and serving.

Store, tightly covered, in the fridge and eat within 4 days.

DIVINE DOUBLE CHOCOLATE CHEESECAKE

The warm spices and orange zest add an extra dimension to the richest of cheesecakes but as well as good chocolate, it's important to choose a good quality cream cheese when you make a cheesecake. Avoid the low-fat and 'bargain' kinds as they contain binders or gums, whereas you need a full-fat type with a good tangy and very slightly salty taste and texture to match the rich chocolate and spices.

MAKES 1 LARGE CHEESECAKE – SERVES 8–12

For the base

225g digestive biscuits
1/4 teaspoon ground cinnamon
a little freshly grated nutmeg
1 x 100g bar Divine orange milk
    chocolate

For the filling

2 x 100g bars Divine dark
    chocolate
400g full-fat cream cheese
2 large free range eggs, beaten
    to mix
50g caster sugar
1 teaspoon vanilla essence
grated zest of 1/2 unwaxed orange
1/4 teaspoon ground cinnamon
a little freshly grated nutmeg
a little freshly ground black
    pepper
200ml double cream
Divine cocoa powder for dusting

23cm springclip tin, greased and
    set on a baking tray

Heat the oven to 170C/325F/Gas 3.

To make the base: put the biscuits, cinnamon and nutmeg into the bowl of a food processor and crush to fine crumbs (or put into a plastic bag and bash with a rolling pin). Break up the orange milk chocolate, put into a large heatproof bowl and melt gently (see page 16). Remove the bowl from the heat and stir in the crumbs.

Tip the mixture into the prepared tin and press onto the base and halfway up the sides of the tin using the back of a spoon. Chill until needed.

To make the filling: break up the dark chocolate, put it into a heatproof bowl and melt gently (see page 16). Remove the bowl from the heat and leave to cool until needed.

Put the cream cheese, eggs, sugar, vanilla, orange zest, cinnamon, a few grates of nutmeg, and a couple of grinds (on the fine setting) of black pepper, into the bowl of a food processor. Run the machine until the ingredients are thoroughly combined, scraping down the sides from time to time. With the machine running, add the cream through the feed tube, followed by the melted chocolate. When smooth and completely blended pour the filling onto the crumb base and spread evenly.

Bake in the heated oven for about 40 minutes or until just firm. Turn off the oven and leave the cheesecake inside to cool down, without opening the door – allow a good 2 hours. Remove the cheesecake from the oven then cover and chill overnight. When ready to serve remove from the tin and dust with cocoa.

Store in the fridge and eat within 5 days.

MOCHA CHEESECAKE

This cheesecake delivers a good hit of both chocolate and coffee, with both ingredients used in the crumb base and the cream cheese filling. It's worth planning ahead as the flavours intensify a day or so after baking.

MAKES 1 LARGE CHEESECAKE — SERVES 8—12

For the base
200g digestive biscuits
100g unsalted butter
2 tablespoons Divine cocoa
  powder
½ teaspoon instant coffee
  powder or granules
3 tablespoons caster sugar

For the filling
1 x 100g bar Divine coffee
  chocolate
700g good quality cream cheese
  (not reduced or low fat types),
  at room temperature
75g caster sugar
1 teaspoon vanilla essence
2 large free range eggs, at room
  temperature
Divine cocoa for dusting

23 cm springclip tin, greased and
  set on a baking tray

Heat the oven to 170C/325F/Gas3.

Make the crust first: crush the biscuits to fine crumbs, either in a food processor or by putting into a plastic bag and bashing with a rolling pin. Melt the butter in a medium-sized pan. Stir in the cocoa powder and coffee and then remove from the heat. Once thoroughly combined stir in the sugar and the biscuit crumbs. Tip the mixture into the prepared tin and, using the back of a teaspoon, press onto the base and about 2cm up the sides. Chill until needed.

To make the filling: break up the chocolate, put into a heatproof bowl and melt very gently (see page 16). Remove the bowl from the heat and leave to cool until needed.

Put the cream cheese into the bowl of a food processor. Add the sugar, vanilla and eggs and process until very smooth. Pour 200ml of the mixture into a measuring jug, add the chocolate and mix thoroughly.

Pour the rest of the filling into the crust and then gently drop the chocolate mixture, a heaped teaspoon or so at a time, into the white filling so it is evenly distributed. Using the handle of a teaspoon, carefully swirl or marble the two mixtures together but avoid over mixing.

Bake in the heated oven for about 40 minutes or until the filling no longer wobbles when the tin is gently shaken, then turn off the oven but leave the cheesecake inside with the door closed to cool down with the oven. When cold, remove the cheesecake, cover the top of the tin tightly then chill overnight. Unclip the tin and set the cheesecake on a serving plate. Dust lightly with cocoa just before serving.

Store in an airtight container in the fridge and eat within 5 days.

MOUSSES

CHILLED DOUBLE CHOCOLATE MOUSSE CAKE

This luxurious dessert is more of a mousse than a cake despite it being baked. The ground almonds give it a wonderful soft fluffy texture. Make a day ahead then serve chilled straight from the fridge with crème fraîche or ice-cream and perhaps a bowl of fresh berries.

MAKES 1 LARGE DESSERT, SERVES 12

1 x 100g bar Divine coffee milk chocolate
3 x 45g bars Divine plain chocolate
250g unsalted butter, diced, very soft
6 large free range eggs, at room temperature
200g caster sugar
100g ground almonds

To serve
Divine cocoa, and icing sugar to dust
Crème fraîche or clotted cream or coffee ice-cream

23cm springclip tin, greased and base-lined

Heat the oven to 200C/400F/Gas 6.

Break up all the chocolate and melt gently (see page 16). Remove the bowl from the heat and stir in the butter. When smooth leave to cool until needed.

Separate the eggs, putting the yolks into the bowl of an electric mixer and the whites into another. Add all but 2 tablespoons of the sugar to the egg yolks and whisk until very thick, pale and foamy. Gradually, on a low speed, whisk in the chocolate mixture. When thoroughly combined mix in the almonds – the mixture will be very thick and heavy.

Whip the egg whites until soft peaks form then whisk in the remaining sugar. Using a large metal spoon, mix a quarter of the egg whites into the chocolate mixture, stirring well to make the mixture softer and looser. Then gently fold in the rest of the egg white mixture in three batches.

Scrape the mixture into the tin and spread evenly. Bake in the heated oven for 25 minutes until there is a firm crust but the centre is still a bit wobbly. Remove the cake from the oven and leave to cool on a wire rack. Cover tightly and chill overnight. When ready to serve, remove from the tin and set on a serving plate. Dust with cocoa then icing sugar and serve with crème fraîche, clotted cream or coffee ice-cream.

Tightly cover and store in the fridge, eat within 5 days.

FRENCH BISTRO CHOCOLATE MOUSSE

This is a lighter, creamy version of the classic mousse but still gives a decent chocolate hit. Serve with thin, crisp biscuits and a glass of Cognac.

SERVES 8

For the decoration
1 x 100g bar Divine dark or white or milk chocolate

For the mousse
2 x 100g bars Divine dark chocolate
2 tablespoons water
4 large free range eggs, at room temperature, separated
225ml double cream, well chilled
2 tablespoons caster sugar

8 glasses or glass dishes

Begin by decorating the glasses – break up half the bar of your chosen decorating chocolate. Put into a heatproof bowl and melt gently (see page 16). Remove the bowl from the heat and spoon the melted chocolate into a greaseproof paper icing bag or a small plastic bag. Snip off the tip of the bag with a pair of kitchen scissors, pipe a swirl of chocolate inside each glass – it should look rather random and quirky, not neat. Chill in the fridge until needed. Grate or shave the rest of the chocolate bar and set aside for the final decoration.

To make the mousse: break up the dark chocolate, put into a large heatproof bowl with the water and melt gently. Remove the bowl from the heat, leave to cool for a couple of minutes then gently stir in the yolks, one at a time. Put the egg whites into the bowl of a food mixer (the bowl must be spotlessly clean and grease-free) and, using the whisk attachment, whip the egg whites until soft peaks form. Whisk in the sugar, and continue for a few seconds until stiff peaks form.

In another bowl, whip the cream until soft peaks form. Using a large metal spoon, gently fold the cream into the chocolate mixture in three batches and then fold in the whites in three batches. Carefully spoon the mixture into the decorated glasses. Chill for at least two hours and up to a day before serving (if chilling overnight cover with cling film). Remove from the fridge about 15 minutes before serving and decorate with the grated chocolate or shavings and leave to 'come to'.

ITALIAN WALNUT, CHOCOLATE AND COFFEE MOUSSE

The Italian chef Aldo Zilli made this mousse for a Fairtrade food party I attended, and it was incredibly popular. I've slightly adapted the method so it can be easily made at home but used all the same delicious ingredients. The taste of the walnuts comes through really well if you make the mousse a day or so before serving.

SERVES 6

2 x 100g bars Divine dark chocolate
100g unsalted butter, diced
2 teaspoons Fairtrade instant coffee powder or granules
3 tablespoons hot water
2 large free range eggs, separated, plus 1 large egg white
2 tablespoons caster sugar
30g walnut pieces, roughly chopped or crushed
50ml whipping or double cream, chilled
walnut halves to decorate

Break up the dark chocolate, put into a heatproof bowl with the butter and melt gently (see page 16). Remove the bowl from the heat, stir gently and leave to cool for a minute.

Dissolve the coffee in the hot water, cool slightly then stir into the chocolate. Stir in the 2 egg yolks. Whisk the 3 egg whites until they form soft peaks then whisk in the sugar. Stir about a quarter of the whites into the chocolate mixture to soften it and then fold this mixture into the remaining egg whites. Finally, whip the cream to soft peaks and fold in, followed by the walnut pieces.

Spoon the delicious mixture into either serving glasses, small espresso-sized coffee cups or a pretty bowl. Decorate with the walnut halves and then cover and chill overnight. Bring out of the fridge 15–20 minutes before serving, to allow the mousse to 'come to', and serve with whipped cream.

ZEBRA MOUSSE

Although simple to make this wonderful Italian black and white chocolate mousse looks impressive. Serve in individual glasses to show the pretty layers of dark chocolate, coffee flavoured white chocolate, and the topping of grated dark chocolate. Serve with crisp biscuits.

SERVES 6

For the dark chocolate mousse
1 x 100g bar Divine dark
  chocolate
100ml double cream
100ml whipping cream, chilled

*For the white chocolate
  mixture*
1 x 100g bar Divine white
  chocolate
100ml double cream
1½ teaspoons Fairtrade instant
  coffee powder or granules
100ml whipping cream, chilled

To finish
1 x 45g bar Divine dark
  chocolate, finely chopped or
  grated

6 glasses for serving

To make the dark chocolate mousse: break up the chocolate and put it into a heatproof bowl and melt gently (see page 16). Remove the bowl from the heat. Gently warm the double cream until it feels the same temperature as the chocolate then gently stir the two together. Leave to cool slightly. Whip the whipping cream until soft peaks form then gently fold into the chocolate mixture. Divide the mixture evenly between the 6 glasses and put into the fridge to chill thoroughly for 1–2 hours.

To make the white chocolate mixture: break up the white chocolate and melt very gently (see page 16). Remove the bowl from the heat and cool slightly. Meanwhile, gently heat the double cream, add the coffee and stir until completely dissolved. Remove from the heat and cool until it feels about the same temperature as the chocolate, whisk the coffee cream into the chocolate to make a smooth mixture (it will darken as you whisk). Leave to cool slightly. Whip the whipping cream until soft peaks form then fold into the coffee chocolate mixture. Spoon the mixture on top of the dark chocolate mixture and return the glasses to the fridge. Chill until firm, about 3–4 hours, or cover and leave overnight.

Just before serving decorate the top of each mousse with the finely chopped chocolate.

CLASSIC CHOCOLATE MOUSSE

This well-loved classic French recipe, using just three ingredients, is wonderful in its simpl... but only works if you use excellent quality chocolate. If you do feel like jazzing it up I've inc... some ideas. It's very rich so only serve individual small portions in pretty glasses rather tha... large bowl.

SERVES 4—6

1 x 100g bar Divine dark chocolate
25g unsalted butter, at room temperature
4 large free range eggs, at room temperature, separated

4–6 glasses or cups

Break up the chocolate, put into a heatproof bowl and melt gently (see page 16). Remove the bowl from the heat. Cut the butter into small pieces and gently stir into the chocolate. Leave to cool for a couple of minutes then gently stir in the egg yolks, one at a time.

Put the egg whites into the spotlessly clean, grease-free bowl of a food mixer. Using the whisk attachment beat until soft peaks form. Using a large metal spoon, stir about a quarter of the whites into the chocolate, mixing quite well to soften the mixture. Then gently fold in the rest of the whites in three batches. Spoon the mousse into the dishes then chill for at least 2 hours before serving. It's best eaten the same day, if you are keeping it overnight make sure you cover the dishes with cling film.

The mousse looks especially good when served in frosted wine glasses – dip the rims of the glasses in lightly beaten egg white then in caster sugar. Leave to set in the fridge while making the mousse.

TRY THIS TOO...

Add two tablespoons of brandy or rum to the broken up chocolate before melting. Serve in brandy balloon glasses.

Or add three tablespoons espresso coffee to the broken up chocolate before melting. Serve in demitasse or espresso coffee cups.

ICE-CREAMS

BITTER ORANGE SOUFFLES GLACES

Individual dark chocolate cases filled with an intensely flavoured orange mousse and frozen; these make the ideal little dessert for guests – you can prepare them ahead and they look divine! No need for an ice-cream machine or churning.

SERVES 6

*3 x 45g bars Divine dark
    chocolate
250ml whipping cream
2 large free range eggs
75g caster sugar
grated zest of 1 unwaxed orange
2 tablespoons orange juice
2 tablespoons orange liqueur
Divine cocoa powder for dusting*

For the caramel sauce
*250g granulated sugar (works
    better than caster)
300ml water*

*clementines for serving – see
    below*

*6 paper muffin cases set in a
    muffin tray*

Clear a space in the freezer for the muffin tray. Place a freezer bowl into the freezer to chill – to be used later.

Break up the chocolate and melt gently (see page 16). Remove the bowl from the heat and leave to cool until very thick and starting to set. Using a pastry brush, thickly coat the inside of the paper cases with the chocolate, using all the chocolate. Leave to set until needed.

Put the cream into chilled bowl and whip until soft peaks form. Chill until needed. Separate the eggs, putting the yolks into the bowl of a food mixer. Add half of the sugar, and the orange zest. Using the whisk attachment beat until the mixture is very thick and pale – about 4 minutes. Set aside until needed. In another bowl whip the egg whites until soft peaks form. Whisk in the remaining sugar.

Add the yolk mixture and the egg whites to the cream and gently fold together using a large metal spoon. When almost combined add the orange juice and the orange liqueur and fold in. Spoon the mixture into the chocolate cases, piling it up well above the rim (if there is any mixture leftover freeze it in a ramekin dish) then freeze until firm – not less than 3 hours but preferably overnight. If freezing for any longer then cover well.

To make the caramel sauce: put the sugar and half the water into a medium-sized heavy pan. Stir over a low heat until the sugar dissolves (don't allow to boil at this point). Once totally dissolved bring the liquid to a boil and boil steadily for about 4–5 minutes, without stirring, until the syrup turns a good deep amber colour (170C/340F on a sugar thermometer). Remove the pan from the heat (to avoid overcooking and burning the caramel), then cover your hand with an oven glove and carefully pour in the remaining water – take care, as the caramel will splutter violently. Put the pan back on a low heat and stir gently until the caramel dissolves. Leave to cool and then pour the caramel over the peeled clementines, cover and chill until needed.

To serve, remove the soufflés from the freezer and gently peel off the paper cases. Set on individual plates and leave in the fridge to 'come to' for about 15 minutes. Dust with cocoa and serve with the caramel sauce and peeled clementines.

ICE-CREAMS

ICED CHOCOLATE TIRAMISU

This tiramisu uses the classic Italian Lady, or sponge fingers (sometimes labelled tiramisu fingers) available from good delis. They are soaked in a coffee and liqueur syrup and then layered with a rich mascarpone mousse. There's no churning or ice-cream making so the whole recipe is delicious yet incredibly easy.

SERVES 6

For the coffee syrup
200ml water
1 tablespoon instant Fairtrade
   coffee powder or granules
150g caster sugar

For the mousse
200ml double cream, well-chilled
250g mascarpone
4 tablespoons coffee liqueur –
   Tia Maria, Kahlua, or Brandy
100g (1/2 packet) Italian lady
   sponge fingers
1 x 100g bar Divine dark
   chocolate

*freezer-proof serving bowl,
   preferably glass*

Heat the water for the syrup in a small pan. Stir in the coffee then the sugar over a low heat then bring to the boil and simmer for 5 minutes until syrupy. Leave to cool, then chill thoroughly. Whip the double cream until soft peaks form. Stir the mascarpone until very smooth then stir into the whipped cream. Gradually stir in 150ml of the chilled coffee syrup. Add the coffee liqueur or brandy.

Break up each sponge finger into 4 pieces and pour over the coffee liqueur syrup, leave to soak. Chop the chocolate finely in a food processor. To assemble the tiramisu put half the soaked sponge fingers in the base of the freezer bowl. Cover with half the mascarpone mousse then scatter over half the chopped chocolate. Arrange the rest of the soaked sponge fingers on top then cover with the remaining mousse. Scatter over the rest of the chopped chocolate then cover the bowl and freeze for 2–3 hours until firm.

If freezing overnight or longer transfer the tiramisu to the fridge 20 minutes before serving to soften enough to scoop.

INTENSE CHOCOLATE SORBET

Deeply flavoured and perfect on a very hot day served with chilled poached pears. Or maybe added to a glass of iced-coffee for an instant pick-me-up.

SERVES 4–6

2 tablespoons Divine cocoa
   powder
300ml water
125g caster sugar
a cinnamon stick
3 x 45g bars Divine dark
   chocolate

Put the cocoa into a heatproof bowl. Add three tablespoons of the water and stir to a smooth paste. Pour the rest of the water into a saucepan with the sugar and cinnamon. Set over a low heat and stir until the sugar has completely dissolved. Bring to the boil then boil steadily for 2 minutes until syrupy. Remove the pan from the heat and pour the syrup onto the cocoa, whisking well to make a smooth liquid. Return the mixture to the pan and bring back to the boil, whisking well.

Remove the pan from the heat, cool for a minute then break up the chocolate and whisk in to make a smooth, melted liquid. Leave to cool then cover and chill thoroughly. Remove the cinnamon stick and pour into an ice-cream machine and churn until frozen. The mixture can also be frozen in a freezer container, stirring frequently until thick and slushy.

Eat within a few days for the best flavour.

TRY THESE TOO...

Add $1/4$ teaspoon chilli flakes to the pan with the sugar. Strain out as you pour the syrup onto the cocoa mix.

Omit the cinnamon, and add a small bunch of fresh mint leaves, remove before adding to the cocoa.

Use Divine dark mint chocolate.

Add 1 tablespoon coffee beans, roughly crushed, to the pan with the sugar. Strain out before adding to the cocoa.

SPECIAL ICE-CREAM CONES

To go with your homemade ice-cream you need something more exciting than ready made ice-cream cones, so melt some more chocolate, get out the pastry brush and start painting.

MAKES 6 CONES

1 x 100g bar Divine dark or white or dark mint chocolate
6 top quality waffle ice-cream cones, medium to large

Break up the chocolate, put it into a heatproof bowl and melt gently. Remove the pan from the heat. Using a pastry brush, paint the insides of the cones with the melted chocolate. Leave them to set in a cool place, or the fridge in hot weather, then use as soon as possible.

ICE-CREAM PARLOUR FROZEN BANANAS

My favourite snack on a hot day. After dipping the frozen bananas in the melted chocolate, sprinkle with chopped walnuts and serve immediately.

MAKES 6

6 medium bananas, firm not soft
2 x 100g bars Divine dark or
*   white chocolate*
25g unsalted butter
50g very finely chopped walnuts

6 bamboo skewers
baking tray lined with waxed or
*   non-stick baking powder*

Chop off the stalk end from each banana but don't peel. Push a skewer up into each banana, just about a quarter of the way up. Peel the bananas, set on the prepared baking tray and freeze overnight or until firm.

Next day, break up the chocolate and put it into a shallow heatproof dish (choose one the length of a banana). Add the butter and melt gently. Remove the dish from the heat and dip the frozen bananas one at a time, holding them by the stick – work quickly as the chocolate will set rapidly – then sprinkle with nuts.

Eat immediately or return the bananas to the lined baking tray and then to the freezer. Eat within 24 hours.

DARK CHOCOLATE RUM CRUNCH

It may be an old recipe but it's still a treat – a rich vanilla cream mixed with caramel crunch, chopped chocolate and a shot of rum (you can leave the rum out if you're making this for children). Serve with a hot chocolate sauce (see page 133) or in chocolate cones (see page 163).

SERVES ABOUT 6

For the ice-cream mixture
300ml double cream
150ml milk
1 vanilla pod, split
4 large free range eggs
2 tablespoons caster sugar
1 to 2 tablespoons rum

For the crunch mixture
85g wholemeal breadcrumbs
4 tablespoons light muscovado
  sugar
1 x 45g bar Divine dark chocolate

baking tin, oiled

To make the ice-cream: put the cream, milk and the vanilla pod, split lengthways, into a medium saucepan – ideally non-stick. Heat very gently until boiling then remove the pan from the heat. Lift out the vanilla pod and scrape the seeds into the cream.

Put the yolks and the sugar into a heatproof bowl and beat well with a wooden spoon until light and creamy. Stir in the hot cream then tip the mixture back into the saucepan. Set over a very low heat and stir constantly until the custard thickens – don't allow it to come close to boiling or it will scramble. Pour into a bowl, stir in the rum and leave to cool then cover and chill thoroughly.

Heat the oven to 200C/400F/Gas 6. Mix the breadcrumbs with the sugar and spread over the base of the oiled tin. Bake in the heated oven for 10–15 minutes, stirring frequently, until a good golden brown. Leave to cool completely then put into a clean plastic bag and crush finely with a rolling pin. Finely chop the chocolate in a food processor and stir into the crumbs.

Pour the chilled ice-cream mixture into an ice-cream machine and churn until almost frozen. Stir in the chocolate crunch mixture and churn for a couple of minutes more until firm. If you don't have a machine, pour the chilled ice-cream mixture into a freezer container and freeze until very slushy, stirring frequently. Stir in the chocolate crunch mixture then cover and freeze until firm.

Best eaten as soon as possible.

ITALIAN FIG AND CHOCOLATE ICE-CREAM

An incredibly easy ice-cream that has a wonderful spicy-rich taste and texture that comes from the soft-dried figs. Made without egg custard but simply using the figs, milk, cream, a little sugar plus a lovely bar of dark chocolate. Try scoops of the ice-cream topped with warm melted chocolate and roasted hazelnuts.

SERVES 4–6

1 x 45g bar Divine dark chocolate
250g soft-dried figs
200ml milk, chilled
3 tablespoons caster sugar
250ml double cream, well-chilled

Break up the chocolate, put into the bowl of a food processor and chop as finely as possible. Tip out into a bowl and set aside. Put the figs into the processor bowl and chop roughly. Add the milk and sugar and process to make a smooth purée.

Whip the cream until soft peaks form then fold in the chopped chocolate and the fig purée. Turn the mixture into the ice-cream machine, if you have one, and churn until frozen. You can also freeze the mixture into a freezer container and freeze until firm.

Best eaten within a few days.

RICHLY DARK CHOCOLATE ICE-CREAM

Really rich and silky smooth, this ice-cream has an intense taste of chocolate rather than cream. It's made with both dark chocolate and cocoa, gently cooked to bring out the full flavour.

SERVES ABOUT 6–8

1 x 45g bar Divine dark chocolate
5 tablespoons Divine cocoa powder
300ml creamy milk
2 large free range eggs
200g caster sugar
1 teaspoon vanilla essence
250ml double cream, well-chilled

Break up the chocolate, put it into a heatproof bowl and melt gently (see page 16). Remove the bowl from the heat and leave to cool until needed. Put the cocoa into a heatproof bowl. Mix in enough of the milk to make a smooth paste. Heat the rest of the milk in a saucepan. Stir the hot milk into the cocoa then tip the mixture back into the pan and cook over a low heat for one minute. Remove from the heat and whisk into the melted chocolate. When absolutely smooth leave to cool completely then cover and chill for an hour.

Put the egg yolks, sugar and vanilla into the bowl of a food mixture and whisk until very light, thick and frothy. Whisk in the chilled chocolate mixture then the chilled cream. Pour into an ice-cream machine and churn until firm. The mixture can also be made without a machine, just pour the mixture into a freezer container and freeze until firm, stirring frequently.

Best eaten as soon as possible.

TRY THESE TOO...

Replace 50ml of the milk with 50ml of cold coffee (choose very strong or espresso).

Add 1 x 45g bar Divine dark chocolate or white chocolate, finely chopped, to the ice-cream mixture just before it freezes.

Replace the vanilla with 1 tablespoon chocolate mint liqueur and add 1 x 100g bar Divine dark mint chocolate, finely chopped, to the ice-cream mixture at the last minute.

Add half a teaspoon ground cinnamon and a quarter of a teaspoon cayenne pepper to the cocoa paste.

WHITE CHOCOLATE
ICE-CREAM

You can make this basic white chocolate ice-cream even yummier by adding some dark chocolate, or, if you prefer, some Fairtrade coffee. I like to serve it scooped in wafer cones (see page 163).

SERVES 4—6

225ml milk
225ml double cream
1 vanilla pod, split lengthways
4 large free range egg yolks
60g caster sugar
3 x 45g bars Divine white chocolate

Put the milk, cream and vanilla into a medium pan, preferably non-stick, and heat gently until just steaming. Remove from the heat and cover the pan, leave to infuse for 30 minutes.

Meanwhile, beat the egg yolks and sugar until pale and creamy then stir in the hot cream and milk mixture. Pour the whole mixture back into the pan and stir over a low heat until thick enough to coat the back of a wooden spoon, don't let the mixture come close to boiling or it will curdle.

Remove the pan from the heat and leave to cool slightly. Break up the chocolate, put into a heatproof bowl and pour over the hot custard, discarding the vanilla pod. Stir gently until smooth. Leave to cool then chill thoroughly. Pour into an ice-cream machine and churn until firm, or put the mixture into a freezer-proof container and freeze, stirring frequently until firm. Eat as soon as possible.

TRY THESE TOO...

DOUBLE CHOCOLATE ICE-CREAM

Make up the ice-cream as above then churn until very thick and slushy but not yet frozen. Finely chop 1 x 100g bar Divine dark chocolate and stir in. Serve with a chocolate sauce (see page 133).

ITALIAN WHITE CHOCOLATE ICE-CREAM

Omit the vanilla but stir a tablespoon of Fairtrade instant coffee powder or granules into the hot milk and cream. There's no need to leave the mixture to infuse, just add to the yolks and sugar mixture and continue as above.

SAVOURY

MEXICAN DAY OF THE DEAD WHITE MOLE

To celebrate the Dia de los Muertos, November 2nd, Mexicans plan huge feasts of special spicy foods and breads, with picnics to the graveyards to visit dead family members. This is one of the so-called 'black and white' dishes – a nutty, spicy pale-coloured sauce thickened with white chocolate – served with chicken and wild rice. The sauce tastes most like a good satay, and made with vegetable stock can be served warm with grilled vegetables as a vegetarian dish.

SERVES 6

For the chicken
6 chicken pieces
1 carrot, peeled and chopped
1 onion, peeled and chopped
1 clove garlic, peeled and chopped
1 bay leaf
4 peppercorns

For the sauce
75g unsalted peanuts
25g blanched almonds
25g walnut pieces
1 thick slice white bread, crusts removed and cubed
15g unsalted butter
2 cloves garlic
1 small onion, peeled and chopped
1 small cinnamon stick, broken up into pieces
1 teaspoon chilli flakes, or to taste
1 x 45g bar Divine white chocolate
salt and pepper to taste
wild rice to serve

Start by cooking the chicken and making the stock. Heat the oil in a deep sauté pan or frying pan. Pat dry the chicken pieces then quickly brown them in the hot oil. Drain off the excess oil. Add the carrot, onion, garlic, bay leaf and peppercorns and enough cold water to barely cover. Bring to the boil and simmer gently for 30 minutes. Turn off the heat and leave to cool. Remove the chicken pieces then bring the cooking liquid to a boil and cook rapidly until well reduced – you will need about 250ml for the sauce (about half the stock). Strain the stock and discard the flavourings, leave to cool until needed. Meanwhile, heat the oven to 180C/350F/Gas 4.

Put the peanuts, almonds, walnuts and cubed bread into an ovenproof dish and toast in the heated oven for 7–10 minutes until just turning colour. Leave to cool then tip into the bowl of a food processor. Add 250ml of the strained stock and run the machine to make a smooth purée.

Melt the butter in a large saucepan, add the garlic, onion, cinnamon and chilli and cook gently for about 10 minutes until soft and fragrant. Tip into the processor bowl onto the nut purée and process again until very smooth. Spoon the purée back into the saucepan and cook gently stirring frequently for a couple of minutes until fairly thick.

Break up the chocolate and stir into the sauce over low heat to make a smooth thick sauce. Taste and season with salt, pepper and more chilli flakes as needed. Add the chicken pieces and reheat gently – if the sauce gets very thick and starts to stick, stir in a little more stock.

Serve hot with the cooked wild rice.

DIVINE   HEAVENLY CHOCOLATE RECIPES

PHEASANT MOLE

This festive Mexican dish should be deliciously spicy rather than red-hot. It includes a complex blend of nuts, seeds, fruit and spices to make a thick, nutty sauce that is traditionally emulsified and enriched with dark chocolate. I've simplified and adapted the recipe as Divine dark chocolate is a bit different to Mexican chocolate which is made with cinnamon and has a rougher texture. I've also used pheasant breasts instead of the usual turkey.

SERVES 6

For the pheasant

6 good pheasant breasts, skinned
1 small carrot, peeled and chopped
1 small onion, peeled and chopped
1 clove garlic, peeled and chopped
1 bay leaf
4 peppercorns

For the sauce

3 tablespoons sultanas
100g unblanched almonds
3 tablespoons sesame seeds
3 tablespoons pumpkin seeds
1 slice stale bread, cubed
2 tablespoons olive oil
1 medium onion, peeled and finely chopped
3 cloves garlic, peeled and finely chopped
1 teaspoon chilli flakes   or to taste
1 teaspoon ground cinnamon
1 x 400g can chopped tomatoes
1 x 45g bar Divine dark chocolate
salt to taste
rice to serve

Put the pheasant pieces into a large pan or casserole along with the carrot, onion, garlic, bay leaf and peppercorns. Add enough cold water to just cover then bring to the boil and simmer very gently until just tender – about 30 minutes. Remove the pan from the heat and leave the pheasant to cool gently in the stock.

Put the sultanas into a small bowl and add 100ml of the stock and leave to soak until needed. Heat the oven to 180C/350F/Gas 4. Put the almonds, sesame seeds, pumpkin seeds and the bread cubes into a heatproof baking dish. Toast in the heated oven for 12 minutes, until just starting to colour, stirring halfway through the cooking time.

Meanwhile, heat the oil in a heavy sauté pan or non-stick frying pan. Add the onion and garlic and cook gently, stirring frequently until very soft – about 10 minutes. Add the chilli flakes and cinnamon, stir well and cook for another couple of minutes then tip in the nut mixture and cook for about 5 minutes until you hear the seeds start to 'pop'. Tip the mixture into the bowl of a food processor. Add the chopped tomatoes and the sultanas with their liquid. Process thoroughly to make a smooth, thick purée. Pour the purée back into the sauté pan or frying pan and cook gently for 3 minutes stirring constantly. Stir in 250ml of the stock then break up the chocolate and stir in. Simmer very gently for about 10 minutes, stirring frequently and adding more stock as needed to prevent the sauce from becoming too thick and sticking to the base of the pan. Taste and adjust the seasonings, adding salt and more chilli or stock again as needed. Add the pheasant pieces and cook gently for another 15 minutes, stirring frequently.

Serve with the cooked rice.

SAVOURY

FILLET OF VENISON WITH A RICH CHILLI AND CHOCOLATE SAUCE

This simple, tasty venison dish when served with rösti potatoes and grilled mushrooms makes the perfect dish for special occasions. The rich sauce gives a robust deep bitter-chocolate, but not sweet taste, enhancing both the tender meat and the chilli sauce. Queen Victoria and her wealthy subjects with clever cooks were very fond of grouse served in a dark and rich wine sauce finished with a small amount of bitter chocolate, so the combination has been around for a long while.

SERVES 4

500g piece venison fillet

For the rösti
500g large potatoes
2 tablespoons chopped parsley
2 tablespoons snipped chives
salt and black pepper to taste
25g unsalted butter

For the mushrooms
4 very large flap-cap mushrooms
25g unsalted butter
salt and black pepper to taste

For the sauce
25g unsalted butter
1 red onion, finely chopped
1 small red chilli, or to taste,
* seeded and finely chopped*
150ml red wine
100ml good game or beef stock
1 bay leaf
sprig of fresh thyme
1 x 45g bar Divine dark
* chocolate, broken up*
salt and black pepper to taste

Place the meat on a plate and pat dry with kitchen paper towels. Leave to come to room temperature before cooking.

Meanwhile, make the rösti: peel and coarsely grate the potatoes. Using your hands (or a clean tea towel) squeeze the potatoes, a handful at a time, to remove as much water as possible. Put the squeezed-dry potatoes into a mixing bowl with the chopped parsley and chives and a little salt and black pepper to taste.

Heat the oven to 150C/300F/Gas 2. Heat the grill ready for the mushrooms.

Heat half the butter for the rösti in a large heavy frying pan (preferably non-stick). Add the potatoes and press down gently to make a neat, even cake. Fry over a medium heat for about 10 minutes, or until the base is very crisp and a good golden brown. Flip the cake over – the easiest way to do this is to place a baking tray over the pan, then invert the pan and the cake so the cake falls onto the tray. Add the rest of the butter to the empty frying pan then slide the cake back into the pan so the cooked side is uppermost. Cook for another 10 minutes or until the underside is also crisp and a good golden brown, and the centre has cooked. Turn the cake out onto a heatproof serving plate and keep in the warm oven. Or you could make 12 wafer-thin rösti by dividing the grated potato mixture into 12 equal portions. Cook 3 at a time, gently spreading out the mixture into thin cakes about 10cm across. Cook for about 5 minutes on each side until a good golden brown. Keep warm in the oven while cooking the remainder. Serve in stacks with the venison.

Wipe the mushrooms with damp kitchen paper but don't wash them. Remove the stalks and save for the sauce. Arrange the mushrooms on the grill pan, dot with butter, season lightly with salt and black pepper then grill for 4–5 minutes on each side until just tender. Keep warm with the rösti.

(Continued on page 176)

(Continued from page 175)

To cook the venison: first lightly season the meat with salt and pepper and heat the butter in a large heavy frying pan. When the butter begins to look foamy add the meat and sear on all sides – allow about $1^1/_2$–2 minutes on each of the four sides for medium rare. Remove from the pan, cover lightly and leave to 'relax' whilst making the sauce.

Add the chopped onion to the pan. Finely chop the mushroom stalks and add with the chilli. Cook, over a medium heat, stirring constantly for about 3 minutes until golden. Add the red wine, stock, bay leaf and thyme and stir well until the mixture comes to the boil. Boil rapidly, stirring frequently until the sauce has reduced by half. Strain the sauce into a clean saucepan. Reheat and taste for seasoning, adding salt and pepper as needed. Remove from the heat and whisk in the chocolate to make a smooth glossy sauce. Taste again and whisk in a knob of butter or more seasoning or even chilli if desired.

Carve the fillet into 4 pieces and serve with the rösti, grilled mushrooms and hot sauce.

COCOA-DUSTED SCALLOPS WITH TAGLIARELLE AND ROCKET

I had seen scallops and tagliarelle on the menus of several well-reviewed restaurants and was intrigued to see if I could slightly adapt it. So, instead of lightly coating the scallops with seasoned flour before searing them in olive oil, I thought I would try using a teaspoon of cocoa powder. The contrast of the bitter cocoa and the sweetness of the scallops plus the peppery rocket and slightly salty pasta really did work. You do need to use a very good flat ribbon type of dried egg pasta such as tagliatelli, pappardelle or tagliarelle.

SERVES 2 AS A MAIN DISH OR 4 AS A FIRST COURSE

175g tagliarelle or tagliatelli
sea salt and freshly ground black pepper to taste
6 large scallops
1 teaspoon Divine cocoa powder
5 tablespoons good olive oil
½ small onion, finely chopped
100g wild rocket, well washed and drained
4 tablespoons hot fish or vegetable stock

Fill a large pan with cold water, add a little salt and bring to the boil. Add the pasta, stir well and cook as directed on the pack.

While the pasta is cooking, rinse the shelled scallops, trim if necessary then slice each in half horizontally, keeping the corals intact. Combine the cocoa with a little salt and pepper then toss the scallops and corals in the mixture so they are just lightly coated.

Heat 2 tablespoons of the oil in a sauté pan or heavy frying pan. Add the scallops and corals and sear briefly, allowing about a minute on each side. Remove from the pan and keep warm. Add another 2 tablespoons of oil to the pan, turn down the heat to low and add the onion. Cook gently, stirring until softened. Tear up the rocket then add it to the pan and toss briefly. Add the hot stock and a little salt and plenty of black pepper then remove the pan from the heat. Drain the pasta, toss with the last spoonful of olive oil then add the rocket sauce. Toss gently then divide between the serving plates. Arrange the scallops on top and eat immediately.

CRAB RISOTTO WITH WHITE CHOCOLATE

Choose Italian risotto rice from the Po valley – Arborio, carnaroli or vialone nano – these have short, stubby grains which stay firm but make a good creamy risotto. You will also need some good fish stock plus white crab meat (freshly cooked if possible but you can also buy it frozen). The white chocolate is added at the end instead of the usual knob of butter. I haven't included the usual final topping of grated Parmesan that risottos have because I don't think it is needed but it's up to you.

SERVES 2 AS A MAIN DISH OR 4 AS A FIRST COURSE

Approximately 650ml good fish stock
½ small onion, finely chopped
1 clove garlic, crushed
2 tablespoons good olive oil
175g risotto rice
1 tablespoon brandy
150g white crabmeat
sea salt and freshly ground black pepper
½ x 45g bar Divine white chocolate, finely chopped
2 tablespoons parsley, finely chopped

Bring the stock to the boil then turn down the heat so it barely simmers. In a heavy pan sweat the onion and garlic in the olive oil until very soft, but not coloured. Add the unwashed rice and stir for a minute. Add the brandy and stir until almost completely evaporated. Add about a third of the hot stock and stir thoroughly over a medium heat. Keep stirring so the rice doesn't stick or burn and keep adding more stock as it is absorbed. The process will take about 20 minutes, (there are no short cuts), and the rice will become creamy and al dente – tender but still with some bite. Add the crab just before the end of the cooking time and then as soon as the rice is cooked to your satisfaction remove the pan from the heat. Season to taste, stir in the white chocolate and the parsley and serve.

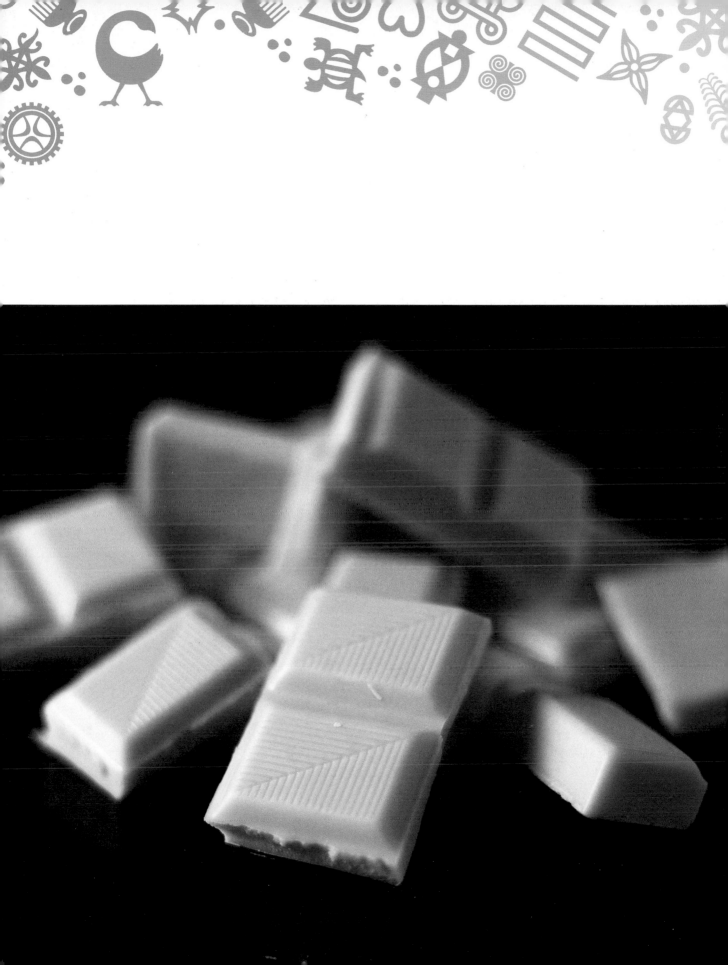

DRINKS & DIPS

HOT MOCHA DIVINE

Incredibly rich, so serve in tiny cups. For this recipe you need to use hot, fresh coffee made from Fairtrade ground beans (using a cafetière or drip machine) rather than instant. For a slightly different flavour try pouring the warm chocolate into warmed Russian-tea glasses, then top up with coffee then add the cream to make three layers.

SERVES 4–6

2 x 100g bars Divine dark chocolate
500ml Fairtrade coffee, strong and hot
150ml whipping cream, well-chilled
2 tablespoons icing sugar
Divine cocoa or drinking chocolate for sprinkling

Break up the chocolate, put into a heatproof bowl and melt gently (see page 16). Remove the bowl from the heat and gradually whisk in the hot coffee to make a smooth thick liquid. Spoon or pour into warmed cups. Whip the cream until soft peaks form then whisk in the sugar. Carefully top the coffee mixture with the cream then sprinkle with cocoa or drinking chocolate and serve immediately.

TRY THIS TOO...   INSTANT MOCHA

Stir 1$\frac{1}{2}$ tablespoons of Divine drinking chocolate into a mug of hot coffee. Top with a spoonful of whipped cream and serve immediately.

THE THICK AND RICH CHOCOLATE SHAKE

Completely indulgent – serve over ice cubes or a scoop of ice-cream.

SERVES 2

1 x 45g bar Divine dark chocolate
1 large, ripe banana
350ml ice cold creamy milk
2 tablespoons Divine drinking chocolate
ice cubes or ice-cream to serve

Break up the chocolate and put into a heatproof bowl, melt gently (see page 16). Remove the bowl from the heat and leave to cool for a minute. Slice the banana into the jug of a food blender or processor. Add the milk and drinking chocolate and run the machine until the mixture is very smooth. Add the melted chocolate and run the machine again until fully combined and frothy.

Spoon a few ice-cubes or a scoop of ice-cream into a couple of chilled glasses and pour over the milkshake. Serve immediately.

REAL AND LUXURIOUS HOT CHOCOLATE

If you've never tasted the real thing you've never lived! For a warm spicy flavour just add a cinnamon stick to the pan with the milk and remove it before serving.

SERVES 2

1 x 100g bar Divine dark chocolate
300ml creamy milk
1 tablespoon caster sugar
100ml whipping cream, whipped
Divine cocoa powder or drinking chocolate for sprinkling

Break up the chocolate and put into a medium-sized pan with the milk and sugar. Heat the chocolate gently over a low heat, stirring frequently until the chocolate has melted, then bring to the boil, whisking constantly until foamy. Pour into warmed mugs, spoon the whipped cream on top and dust with cocoa or drinking chocolate. Serve immediately.

SANDERSON'S DIVINITINI

This amazing, and very popular, cocktail was created by the barman of the ultra-chic Sanderson Hotel, in the west-end of London. It's normally only available in the Purple Bar to residents, where it's served in chilled martini glasses garnished with a purple pansy!

For each cocktail

*4 squares of Divine milk
   chocolate, melted
1 fl oz Wyborowa orange vodka
1 fl oz pure vodka
a dash of Grand Marnier
a dash of Crème de Cacao
1 slice orange*

*To garnish – a purple pansy, if
   desired!*

Put the melted chocolate, orange vodka, pure vodka, Grand Marnier, Crème de Cocoa into a cocktail shaker. Crush the orange slice and add. Shake well and then pour into a chilled glass, decorated with a pansy on the side, and sip.

A TRIO OF CHOCOLATE DIPS

This has the easiest and best of all treats – three kinds of chocolate, melted with cream plus wonderful fruit and cake for dipping.

SERVES ABOUT 6

choose 3 x 100g bars of Divine chocolate – dark, white, milk, or coffee chocolate, orange chocolate, hazelnut or dark mint

Break up each chocolate bar, put into separate heatproof bowls and melt very gently (see page 16). Remove the bowls from the heat. Heat 125ml double cream until very hot but not quite boiling then gently stir an equal amount into each bowl of melted chocolate. If you want you can also add a tablespoon of a suitable liquor – dark or Bacardi rum, brandy, Grand Marnier, Tia Maria, Kahlua.

If possible set the bowls on a warming tray and serve with a platter of prepared fruits – whole strawberries and cherries, chunks of banana, physalis fruit, wedges of fresh pineapple, plus sponge fingers or madeleines (see page 54), amaretti biscuits and marshmallows for dipping.

INDEX